Pediatric assessment of self-care activities

Pediatric assessment of self-care activities

Ida Lou Coley, O.T.R.

Head, Department of Occupational Therapy
Children's Hospital at Stanford
Palo Alto, California

with 54 illustrations

art work by Mary K. Shrader

The C. V. Mosby Company

Saint Louis   1978

The C. V. Mosby Company
11830 Westline Industrial Drive, St. Louis, Missouri 63141

Library of Congress Cataloging in Publication Data

Coley, Ida Lou, 1927-
    Pediatric assessment of self-care activities.

    Bibliography: p.
    Includes index.
    1. Child development—Testing. 2. Autonomy
(Psychology). I. Title. [DNLM: 1. Activities of
daily living—In infancy and childhood. 2. Child
development. 3. Motor skills—In infancy and childhood.
WS103 C695p]
RJ50.C64   155.4   77-22529
ISBN 0-8016-1022-2

GW/CB/CB 9 8 7 6 5 4 3 2

for
GLADYS CRUSON COLEY

Preface

Independence is both functionally and symbolically important in life in the United States. For the individual it denotes, among other things, the state of being self-reliant, separate from, autonomous.

This handbook describes how a child attains independence in self-care. It presents an assessment for measuring the child's sufficiency in activities of daily living appropriate to his developmental status. To analyze the growth of his self-direction and action, an examination is made of behaviors that precede and/or affect independence. The most detailed account records motor behavior. An outline of developmental sequences traces neuromotor development from birth through early childhood as the child progresses toward independence in care tasks.

The handbook stresses that a child's independence is also influenced by other growth processes, more difficult to identify. One of these is socialization—his interaction with other human beings. Additionally, independence is actuated by the social system in which the child lives and the way culture deals with the processes of daily living. Tools, games, and jobs become part of the tasks to be mastered. The competency with which the child accomplishes tasks and progresses in skill building is affected by his sensory awareness and his ability to perceive information about the environment and to interpret his perceptions. Thus growth in independence becomes complex to analyze.

The multiple facets of development that shape independence necessitate a systematic and orderly method of recording time-related aspects of task accomplishment. A particular tool, an activities of daily living assessment form, is designed to give a sequential order by which tasks are mastered and a chronological time span over which the quality of performance can be measured. The computer age requires that data be specific and retrievable.

As the text progresses, it expands beyond the technical aspects of data collection and those components of behavior readily accessible to observation. Conclusive pages include an overview of the assessment process in its entirety and emphasize the importance of clarity and simplicity in communicating the results of the assessment to others.

The handbook has been prepared with the student in mind. It is intended to meet the needs of students immersed in the work of organizing didactic information into a practical form that can be applied in working with patients. Its purpose is to aid the student or new therapist in identifying strengths and deficits in daily life function from birth through childhood. The arrangement of the material throughout the text parallels a student's professional growth from observer and recorder to participator-activator, interpreter, and consultant.

The handbook hopefully will foster the acquisition of certain abilities on the part of the user. It seems reasonable to predict that as an assessor acquires a clearer understanding of how independence in daily living evolves in the infant and child, he becomes more astute in identifying gaps in development and in detecting the presence of maladaptive patterns of coping with the environment. He gains a clearer focus in determining which skills need the attention of therapy procedures and in what order. He becomes a collector of specific data while appreciating the complexity of the assessment process and its professional nature.

Although the handbook does not focus on symptoms and manifestations of disease and disability that limit the child's performance, it does provide a system of measurement that enables an assessor to recognize areas of deficiency and strength. Most conspicuously the text is limited to highlighting growth and change in the maturation process. To make the best use of the material presented here, the reader should study the references listed for further detail.

Readers may include others from the allied health professions in addition to students of occupational and physical therapy. In the clinical field we share our findings and collective expertise to help the child and his family attain his inherent potential. I hope that this handbook will further contribute to our mutual goals.

Thanks to the following companies for permitting their books to be used as source material in preparing the illustrations for Chapter 4: Columbia University Press, New York; Harper and Row, Publishers, Inc., Hagerstown, Md.; Churchill Livingstone, Edinburgh, Scotland; Plenum Publishing Corporation, New York; W. B. Saunders Company, Philadelphia; Charles C Thomas, Publisher, Springfield, Ill.

I am deeply indebted to a number of individuals who have contributed significantly to the effort of producing the handbook. Dr. Harry Jennison, Dr. Eugene Bleck, and Dr. Elizabeth Richards provided support and guidance in improving assessment procedures. Various staff members read portions of the text and offered suggestions: Claudia Brower Brown, Setsu Marshall, Fran Ford, Dr. Steven Lazoff, Dr. Pauline Adams, Beth Harper, Kay Stricklan, and Dr. Chester Swinyard. Interest and assistance in preparing the manuscript were given by Lorna van Lankeren, Betty Boston and Florence Fujimoto. Rolf Henrik Schroeder supplied counsel and generous encouragement.

Ida Lou Coley

Contents

APPENDIXES

Pediatric assessment of self-care activities

1 *Characteristics of assessment*

To effectively administer an assessment and interpret findings, an assessor should be familiar with the qualities that distinguish the assessment process.

DEFINITION

Assessment can be defined as an observational study of a subject carrying out specific tasks. It requires data collection on the performance and an analysis about the degree and amount of discrepancy from normal function. For purposes of this handbook, it also includes a consideration of how activities of daily living contribute to personal satisfaction and their effect on productivity in school, work, and play. The assessor notes how the level of function facilitates or hinders progress in appropriate, related developmental tasks. Data provide a basis for constructing a plan. Specific recommendations may cover suggested actions to be carried out by the assessor and/or other interested parties.

PURPOSE AND GENERAL PHILOSOPHY

The purpose of an assessment and a general philosophy of its use merge into one when viewed in the context of this handbook. Pearson and Williams (1972) suggest a workable bonding. The first philosophical principle is that an assessment in self-care is for the purpose of determining "*what* the child can do and *why* he can do some things and not others." This statement establishes that identifying abilities is equally as important as identifying deficits and that recording results is not sufficient. The determination of reasons for function and nonfunction is a part of assessing performance, signifying a positive approach, a recognition that every individual has a degree of potential, limited though it may be. The goal of assessment should be to identify that potential, explain it, cultivate it, and use it to a maximum in dealing with existing limitations. Such an approach presents help in addition to prediction. The value extends not only to the child but to his family as well. Attention is focused beyond the diagnosis to a plan for an effective ongoing program of which the family becomes a part in some measure.

The second philosophical principle is that assessment should be carried out at an early age. The reasons for this will emerge from a study of development. Most obvious is the plasticity that exists in the infant and young child. For example, there is greater success in interrupting abnormal motor patterns at an early age.

Moreover, as Pearson and Williams (1972) emphasize, a child's development in intellectual and emotional function is affected by the kind of sensory and motor experiences provided from birth.

The third principle is that assessment should not be limited to a single encounter but rather should be repeated at intervals. A child is a rapidly changing organism, and as he grows, his environment also changes. His abilities and limitations assume a different significance at various life stages for him and his family as well as for society at large (Holt, 1966; Pearson and Williams, 1972). An assessment, when viewed in its totality, considers the forces that affect life-style expression and achievement of developmental tasks as the child passes from one stage to another.

Serial assessment also serves the important purpose of validating the success or failure of a treatment program. It may also prophylactically avert a crisis and serve to alert or reassure the family that the program is effective or needs changing.

BOUNDARIES

The boundaries of an assessment can be drawn when its distinct characteristics are described. Banus (1971) distinguishes three types of assessment: the informal, formal, and standardized. An informal assessment gives a general overview of the child's performance and is made through observation in a nonstructured manner. The standardized assessment, on the other hand, is highly structured with strict procedures as to presentation, timing, and scoring. Normative data, gathered from the testing of a sample of children, are used for grading performance.

An activities of daily living assessment fits the criteria of the formal assessment as described by Banus. It is organized for a structured presentation. Individual tasks are chosen to elicit specific, identifiable behavior. Items are selected from standardized tests and informal observations to make up a list of tasks that can be reassessed at intervals.

The boundaries of assessment procedures likewise vary, depending on the type of assessment being conducted. In a standardized assessment, boundaries are clearly defined. The assessor's role is limited to that of an observer and recorder, and both time and place are regulated. An activities of daily living assessment, on the other hand, has flexible boundaries. The assessor may become an active participant in the assessment process and assume a helper role. This may be likened to the process-oriented relationship described by Sattler (1974), whereby during the workup factual information is sought but allowed to emerge in the context of the assessor-child relationship. Without strict boundaries the assessor is free to explore what factors enhance performance and exercise more latitude in drawing out potential.

SUMMARY

A review of the characteristics of assessment is useful in setting the course the procedure should follow. In carrying out an activities of daily living assessment, the assessor follows a structure but exercises flexibility in exploring ways to enhance the child's function. The assessor's role includes not only recording function but explaining it.

REFERENCES

Banus, B. S. 1971. The developmental therapist. Thorofare, N.J., Charles B. Slack, Inc.

Holt, K. 1966. The handicapped child, Proc. Roy. Soc. Med. 59:134-150.

Pearson, P. H., and Williams, C. E., editors. 1972. Physical therapy services in the developmental disabilities. Springfield, Ill., Charles C Thomas, Publisher.

Sattler, J. M. 1974. Assessment of children's intelligence. Philadelphia, W. B. Saunders Co.

2 Activities of daily living assessment

BACKGROUND

An activities of daily living assessment is a traditional tool of the physical and occupational therapist. Wolf (1969) reports that one of the first known checklists of daily life activities for the disabled was devised by Marjorie P. Sheldon and published in 1935. Introduced as a rehabilitation procedure during World War II, it has long served to call attention to the degree of skill and amount of effort required for an individual to function independently in his home and community. As a baseline study, it assists in setting goals for the rehabilitation process, records progress toward those goals, and documents the level of recovery of function.

Throughout the United States, Canada, and other countries, treatment centers have designed their own assessment forms to meet the needs of their particular caseloads and treatment programs. The effort to upgrade, perfect, and broaden the tool continues as an ongoing process. The principle of graphically illustrating levels of function in a time-oriented way has been present from the inception of the idea of activities of daily living and is well suited for the computer age. But the tool has not yet assimilated and used some of the richly explanatory information about child growth appearing in the literature over the last decade, and the need to rebuild the tool so that more discreet judgments can be made about the rapidly developing child is evident to all therapists seeking increased professional competence.

REFINING THE TOOL FOR PEDIATRIC APPLICATION

There are a number of questions to be considered in revising the assessment: "How can maturational milestones be incorporated into the assessment? How many tasks should be included in the assessment? What kind of standards should be set for the performance? Can the assessment be compiled in such a way that each member of the health team will understand the requirements for each task? What kind of symbols can be utilized so that results can be easily interpreted, with minimum effort, by all members of the health team not just by the therapist preparing the report?"

A system of data collection evolved from a design project undertaken by the occupational therapy department at Children's Hospital at Stanford, California, which reflects clear sequential development consistent with the maturation of the central nervous system. The arrangement of data allows the assessment to flow in concert with the appearance and integration of primitive reflexes and the evolution of more advanced patterns of movement. The plan for organizing the data collection in this handbook emerged from the analysis of each task of the activities of daily living assessment as a neuromotor developmental process, beginning with the newborn infant. The results of this approach yield unexpected clarity as the developmental relationships between function, reflexes, and reactions unfold. The approach enables the therapist to see the prerequisites necessary for acquiring skills of daily living. As the tasks are broken down into developmental sequences, it becomes possible to define the task or activity of daily living by drawing from the description of the developmental sequence most closely associated with the level of independence being sought for the task.

An outline of motor skills to be monitored by the occupational therapist is useful in determining the scope of the assessment and indicating appropriate parameters for activities of daily living. Table 1 illustrates the grouping of activities contained in the assessment with a list of motor skills devised by Sukiennicki (1971). Such an inventory does not preclude other evaluations that may precede the activities of daily living assessment or become relevant as a result of it. Examples include joint range measurement; muscle strength examination; sensory evaluation

Table 1. List of motor developmental tasks to be monitored by the occupational therapist and related activities of daily living*

Motor development tasks	Activities of daily living (Children's Hospital at Stanford, Calif.)
Head control	Bed: supine to sitting supported
Eye fixation and following	Reaching: midline
Sucking and swallowing	Feeding
Ingestion of solids	Feeding
Gross arm movements	Reaching: to midline, head, back, toes
Eye-hand coordination	Finger foods
Trunk control	Reaching
Emerging grasp patterns	Utensils
Propping and equilibrium reactions in sitting	Sitting, reaching
Refinement of grasp patterns	Dressing (manipulation, as in fastenings)
	Other assessments
Sensory discrimination	Ayres: Sensory Integration
Later	
Higher equilibrium reactions	Brower Brown: Functional Development
Perceptual motor development	Ayres: Sensory Integration

*Data from Sukiennicki, D. A. 1971. Neuromotor development. In Banus, B. S.: The developmental therapist, p. 195. Thorofare, N.J., Charles B. Slack, Inc.

including touch, superficial pain, thermal factors, and pressure; position sense; stereognosis; body scheme; gross visual fields; and mass pattern motion as opposed to isolated control. In most instances a variety of assessments is desirable to validate findings and to explain the level of function.

From the numerous tasks of daily living, a basic unit of activities is selected and each activity is defined. The normal sequence of behaviors is organized by using the approximate chronological age at which the child accomplishes the defined task. The numerical figures thus serve to maintain the order of the data, and additionally, the chronological system serves as a guide in determining the normative levels of performance. But to focus on specific ages in a rigid way will produce an oversimplified dichotomy of maturation. Each child develops at his own rate within a general pattern of development and in the process is strongly influenced by his experience and environment. Authorities from whom the outline material has been gathered differ in their schedule rates, but if milestones are viewed generally, there is reasonable agreement. Currently, researchers are shifting emphasis from normative levels per se to the relationship between a level of performance and its behavioral antecedents, for example, the type and degree of sensory input (White, Castle, and Held, 1971).

REVIEW OF NEUROMOTOR DEVELOPMENT

Of greater significance than the chronological figures is the sequence of development. Briefly, the process begins in the human embryo with the formation of cells, some of which will become tissues of the central nervous system. Yet at birth this complex network of delicate, interlaced nerve cells is not fully mature and organized. Although the number of nerve cells is complete, totaling some 100 billion, functional connections between them are not totally established, particularly at the highest level of the brain, the cortex. The newborn's response to sensory stimulation then is involuntary in nature. Responses are controlled through reflexes that affect his posture and movement patterns as well as vital functions; for example, initially the infant sucks, swallows, and urinates on a reflexive basis.

A reflex can be defined as an involuntary response to stimulus. In its simplest form it exists as a reflex arc, a neural pathway between the point of stimulation, a center in the brain or spinal cord, and the responding organ, which may be a muscle or gland. Most reflexes, however, are more complicated with their pathways running between a greater number of nerve cells. Reflexes have individual names, such as the Moro reflex or the rooting reflex. They are also classified into groups. Some remain evident throughout life; others are transitory, become integrated, and under most circumstances are not seen after a specified age.

The distinction between a "reflex" and a "reaction" is confusing in the literature, and neurologists may differ in classifying a response as one or the other. Barbara Lohrey (1972), a physical therapist trained in neurodevelopmental treatment, has suggested as a possibility the following description:

> A reflex is a specific stereotyped response to a given stimulus which will usually remain constant in both intensity and response pattern under repeated stimulation.

A reaction, on the other hand, is not stereotyped in that the response may differ from one individual to another or in the same individual at a different moment in time. A reaction can be easily modified and will usually diminish or even disappear with repeated stimulation.*

As the infant's nervous system matures and more connections are established to and between nerve cells at the higher levels in the brain, the higher centers apparently take up the work of inhibiting some of the early primitive reflex patterns affecting posture. At the same time the infant acquires a normal postural reflex mechanism made up of righting, equilibrium, and other adaptive and protective reactions. Bobath (1966) explains that the development of these reactions is closely associated with a normal postural tone which allows for the maintenance of position against gravity and the performance of normal movement. The result is that the infant can exhibit more discrete and selective voluntary movement. For example, by acquiring equilibrium, he has the ability to adjust to changes in his center of gravity so that gradually his arms and hands are freed for manipulatory duty rather than serving as balancing props. By the time of approaching childhood, the primitive reflexes are integrated, forming a substrata for voluntary movement (Sukiennicki, 1971).

The renowned investigator, Arnold Gesell (Gesell and Amatruda, 1947) has established that development yields to diagnosis, that it is organized, beginning before birth, and that the general direction of this organization is head to foot (cephalocaudal) and near to remote (proximal to distal). The Bobaths teach that each new motor activity which emerges is built on previous patterns which are gradually elaborated and modified. These developmental principles are illustrated by a study of the infant's progression of function in activities of daily living. However, not all aspects of performance in these activities fall into a highly predictable pattern. Those involving personal-social behavior such as feeding, toileting, hygiene, and dressing are sensitive to environmental influences. Gesell (1940) points out that personal-social behavior, like postural behavior, follows a maturational sequence, but it does not cling to this sequence steadfastly and with precision. Thus assessors should always remain open to adjusting established schedules and avoid the fallacy of a timetable approach to developmental tasks. For example, present clinical experience is altering the milestones established for bowel and bladder control, extending figures upward to 5 and 6 years of age, with cultural factors exerting a strong influence in determining when actual control is established, even though neurophysiologically the potential may begin to develop from 18 months.

Acknowledgment should also be given to the impact of sensory stimuli on the child's central nervous system and his learning process. In the Eleanor Clarke Slagle Lecture, Mary Fiorentino (1974) incorporates learning theories in noting that it is through sensory stimuli that the child "perceives." He receives sensory information through auditory, gustatory, olfactory, visual, tactile, and proprioception sensory modalities. The sensations are fed into the central nervous system

*From Lohrey, B. 1972. Pediatric care course: analysis and treatment of motor problems in cerebral palsy, San Mateo, Calif., Northern California Physical Therapy Association, Area III, RMP.

and with repetition of an act, the response becomes ingrained, gradually reaching a level of automation until a pattern of behavior, or a learned response, develops. At a later stage cognition, perception plus memory, will play an increasingly important role in the learning process.

Gesell (1940) describes with amusing accuracy that the child in much of his behavior learns backward rather than forward. He undresses before he dresses and takes food out of his mouth before he puts it in. As a therapist, it is always desirable to be alert to humorous subtleties of life and to cultivate an appreciation for the uniqueness of each child and his style of coping.

REFERENCES

Ayres, A. J. 1972. Southern California Sensory Integration Tests. Los Angeles, Western Psychological Services.

Brown, C. B. 1975. In Bleck, E. E., and Nagel, D. A., editors: Physically handicapped children: a medical atlas for teachers, pp. 69-88. New York, Grune & Stratton, Inc.

Bobath, K. 1966. The motor deficit in patients with cerebral palsy. London, William Heinemann, Ltd.

Fiorentino, M. R. 1975. Occupational therapy: realization to activation, 1974 Eleanor Clarke Slagle Lecture, Am. J. Occup. Ther. 29:15-21.

Gesell, A. 1940. The first five years of life—a guide to the study of the pre-school child. New York, Harper & Row, Publishers.

Gesell, A., and Amatruda, C. 1947. Developmental diagnosis, ed. 2, New York, Harper & Row, Publishers.

Lohrey, B. 1972. Pediatric care course: analysis and treatment of motor problems in cerebral palsy, San Mateo, Calif., Northern California Physical Therapy Association, Area III, RMP.

Sukiennicki, D. A. 1971. Neuromotor development. In Banus, B. S.: The developmental therapist. Thorofare, N.J., Charles B. Slack, Inc.

White, B. L., Castle, P., and Held, R.: Observations on the development of visually directed reaching, In Knopp, C., editor: Readings in early development. Springfield, Ill., Charles C Thomas, Publisher.

Wolf, J. M. 1969. The results of treatment in cerebral palsy. Springfield, Ill., Charles C Thomas, Publisher.

3 *Activities of daily living assessment form*

BASIC UNIT OF ACTIVITIES

The assessment form consists of seventy-six defined tasks in activities of daily living. Appendixes of the handbook contain tables listing definitions and references.

A thorough familiarity with the form should precede its use. This includes understanding all terms used on the form, noting how the data are arranged, verifying the definition for each task of daily living, and knowing the symbols for grading the performance. In addition, an assessor should have confidence in his ability to select the appropriate grade for measuring the performance of each task. Guidelines are presented in Chapter 7.

CLARIFICATION OF TERMS

"Time-oriented record" refers to the process of recording data at time intervals, provided on the form by eight columns under the title "Visit number," so that the data can be compared to determine progress. "Julian date" comes from the Julian calendar, introduced in 46 B.C. by Julius Caesar. A Julian date is the numerical figure for a date. For example, February 1 would be "32," February 2, "33," etc. For computer purposes the Julian date provides easier processing.*

Extending horizontally to the right of "Yr. Mo." are spaces in which the age of the child should be recorded. Vertically below "Yr. Mo." there is a subtitle, "Order of dev. seq." (developmental sequence), which is the approximate chronological age at which a child achieves independence in the defined activity of daily living. The initials R. L. extending horizontally to the right of "Order of dev. seq." is a heading for columns where right and left extremity are involved alternately in the activity. Some items may only require a recording for the dominant extremity.

Each activity of daily living is numbered in the column to its left. On the back

---

*The recognized value of computers in conducting research supports the existing need for data collection systems where information is retrievable, consistent in format, and measurable. Such a format, the time-oriented record, has been described in the literature by Fries (1974). Potential areas for study, utilizing computerized data, include prognosis for function and efficacy of programs in improving function.

9

CHILDREN'S HOSPITAL AT STANFORD

ACTIVITIES OF DAILY LIVING ASSESSMENT *

Name of patient _____ Hospital no. _____

Diagnosis _____ Onset _____

Birth date _____

Sex: M   F   Handedness: R   L

	Assessor's signature	**Date**
1.		
2.		
3.		
4.		
5.		
6.		
7.		
8.		

Subtests utilized:

Basic ADL	Communication	Adolescent self-care	Transfers
Wheelchair	Household activities	Equipment list	

*From Bleck, E. E., and Nagel, D. A., editors: Physically handicapped children: a medical atlas for teachers, New York, 1975, Grune & Stratton, Inc. By permission.

	CHILDREN'S HOSPITAL AT STANFORD OCCUPATIONAL THERAPY TIME-ORIENTED RECORD ACTIVITIES OF DAILY LIVING ASSESSMENT
addressograph stamp	

Key to scoring: 4 . . . Independent
                   3 . . . Independent with equipment and/or adaptive technique
                   2 . . . Completes but cannot accomplish in practical time
                   1 . . . Attempts but requires assistance or supervision to complete
                   0 . . . Dependent—cannot attempt activity
                   — . . . Nonapplicable

The **Year-Month** vertical column represents the | Order of developmental sequence | or approximate age when the child accomplishes the activity; the horizontal column represents the chronological age of the child being assessed.

	Visit number		1		2		3		4		5		6		7		8	
	Julian date																	
		Yr. Mo.																
	BED	Order of dev. seq.	R.	L.	R.	L.	R.	L.	R.	L.	R.	L.	R.	L.	R.	L.	R.	L.
1	Supine position	Birth																
2	Prone position	Birth																
3	Roll to side	1-4 wk.																
4	Roll prone to supine	0.6																
5	Roll supine to prone	0.7																
6	Sit up	0.10																
7	Propped sitting	0.6																
8	Sitting/hands props	0.7																
9	Sitting unsupported	0.10-0.12																
	Reaching																	
10	To midline	0.5																
11	To mouth and face	0.6																
12	Above head	—																
13	Behind head	—																
14	Behind back	—																
15	To toes	1.3																
	FEEDING																	
16	Swallow (liquids)	Birth																
17	Drooling under control	1.0																
18	Suck and use straw	2.0																
19	Chew (semisolids, solids)	1.6																
20	Finger foods	0.10																

ACTIVITIES OF DAILY LIVING

Continued.

	CHILDREN'S HOSPITAL AT STANFORD OCCUPATIONAL THERAPY
	TIME-ORIENTED RECORD
	ACTIVITIES OF DAILY LIVING ASSESSMENT

Key to scoring: 4 . . . Independent
3 . . . Independent with equipment and/or adaptive technique
2 . . . Completes but cannot accomplish in practical time
1 . . . Attempts but requires assistance or supervision to complete
0 . . . Dependent—cannot attempt activity
— . . . Nonapplicable

The **Year-Month** vertical column represents the | Order of developmental sequence | or approximate age when the child accomplishes the activity; the horizontal column represents the chronological age of the child being assessed.

	Visit number		1		2		3		4		5		6		7		8	
		Yr. Mo.																	
	FEEDING—cont'd	Order of dev. seq.	R.	L.	R.	L.	R.	L.	R.	L.	R.	L.	R.	L.	R.	L.	R.	L.
	Utensils																		
21	Bottle	0.10																	
22	Spoon	3.0																	
23	Cup	1.6																	
24	Glass	2.0																	
25	Fork	3.0																	
26	Knife	6.0-7.0																	
	TOILETING																		
27	Bowel control	1.6																	
28	Bladder control	2.0																	
29	Sit on toilet	2.9																	
30	Arrange clothing	4.0																	
31	Cleanse self	5.0																	
32	Flush toilet	3.3-5.0																	
	HYGIENE																		
33	Turn faucets on/off	3.0																	
34	Wash/dry hands/face	4.9																	
35	Wash ears	8.0																	
36	Bathing	8.0																	
37	Deodorant	12.0-																	
38	Care for teeth	4.9																	
39	Care for nose	6.0																	

CHILDREN'S HOSPITAL AT STANFORD
OCCUPATIONAL THERAPY

TIME-ORIENTED RECORD

ACTIVITIES OF DAILY LIVING ASSESSMENT

Key to scoring: 4 . . . Independent
3 . . . Independent with equipment and/or adaptive technique
2 . . . Completes but cannot accomplish in practical time
1 . . . Attempts but requires assistance or supervision to complete
0 . . . Dependent—cannot attempt activity
— . . . Nonapplicable

The **Year-Month** vertical column represents the Order of developmental sequence or approximate age when the child accomplishes the activity; the horizontal column represents the chronological age of the child being assessed.

	Visit number	Yr. Mo. Order of dev. seq.	1 R.	1 L.	2 R.	2 L.	3 R.	3 L.	4 R.	4 L.	5 R.	5 L.	6 R.	6 L.	7 R.	7 L.	8 R.	8 L.
	HYGIENE—cont'd																	
40	Care for hair	7.6																
41	Care for nails	8.0																
42	Feminine hygiene	Puberty																
	UNDRESSING																	
	Lower body																	
43	Untie shoe bow	2.0-3.0																
44	Remove shoes	2.0-3.0																
45	Remove socks	1.6																
46	Remove pull-down garment	2.6																
	Upper body																	
47	Remove pull-over garment	4.0																
	DRESSING																	
	Lower body																	
48	Put on socks	4.0																
49	Put on pull-down garment	4.0																
50	Put on shoe	4.0																
51	Lace shoe	4.0-5.0																
52	Tie bow	6.0																
	Upper body																	
53	Put on pull-over garment	5.0																

Continued.

**CHILDREN'S HOSPITAL AT STANFORD
OCCUPATIONAL THERAPY**

TIME-ORIENTED RECORD

ACTIVITIES OF DAILY LIVING ASSESSMENT

Key to scoring: 4 . . . Independent
3 . . . Independent with equipment and/or adaptive technique
2 . . . Completes but cannot accomplish in practical time
1 . . . Attempts but requires assistance or supervision to complete
0 . . . Dependent—cannot attempt activity
— . . . Nonapplicable

The **Year-Month** vertical column represents the | Order of developmental sequence | or approximate age when the child accomplishes the activity; the horizontal column represents the chronological age of the child being assessed.

Visit number			1	2	3	4	5	6	7	8
		Yr. Mo.								
	FASTENERS	Order of dev. seq.								
	Unfastening									
54	Button: front	3.0								
55	side	3.0								
56	back	5.6								
57	Zipper: front	3.3								
58	separating front	3.6								
59	back	4.9								
60	Buckle: belt	3.9								
61	shoe	3.9								
62	Tie: back sash	5.0								
	Fasten									
63	Button: large front	2.6								
64	series	3.6								
65	back	6.3								
66	Zipper: front, lock tab	4.0								
67	separating	4.6								
68	back	5.6								
69	Buckle: belt	4.0								
70	shoe	4.0								
71	insert belt in loops	4.6								
72	Tie: front	6.0								
73	back	8.0								
74	necktie	10.0								
75	Snaps: front	3.0								
76	back	6.0								
	Assessor's initials:									

ACTIVITIES OF DAILY LIVING

of each sheet of the form, ruled lines provide space where the assessor may add comments about performance of an activity, using its number.

REFERENCE

Fries, J. F. 1974. Alternatives in medical record formats, Med. Care **12:**871-881.

4 *Sequences of development leading to independence in self-care tasks*

BED
Supine position
(ability to lie on back)

Developmental sequence: birth

YR. MO.

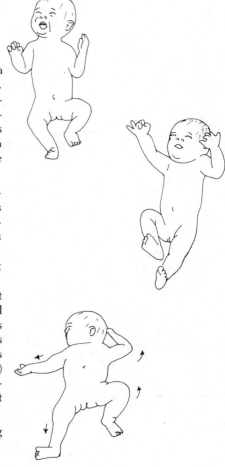

Birth   Hypertonus of flexor muscles with symmetrical distribution is present. Shoulders are adducted, hands are fisted with thumbs adducted, hips are abducted, and ankles are dorsiflexed. This position is derived from position in utero. No equilibrium reactions are present.

Moro reflex is strong, causing an abductor-extensor reaction to various parts of body with movements of supporting surface or shaking of infant's head as in tipping infant backward. Asymmetrical tonic neck reflex is not conspicuous.

0.2   Asymmetrical posture may be present intermittently because of asymmetrical tonic neck reflex, but this posture is not sustained. This reflex produces extensor tone in arm and leg of limbs to which face is turned (face limb) and flexor tone in arm and leg of opposite side (skull limbs). It is strongest at 2 months of age.

Arm and leg movements are becoming more forceful.

Supine position—cont'd

YR. MO.

Extensor tone is increasing while predominant flexor tone of limbs of upper extremities begins to lessen, to be followed by lessening in lower extremities.

0.3 Vigorously kicks legs, showing rapid flexor extensor movements bilaterally or alternately (reciprocal kicking). Moro reflex is less brisk. Hands are loosely open.

0.4 Symmetrical posture is present with absence of asymmetrical tonic neck reflex. Head is held predominantly in midline under influence of symmetrical tonic neck reflex. This reflex produces extension of arms and flexion of legs when head is raised and flexion of arms and extension of legs when head is lowered. Infant engages hands frequently.

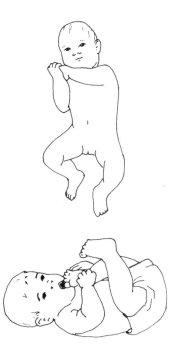

0.6 Massive patterns of flexion and extension are diminishing. Can grasp feet and may bring them to mouth.

0.7 Equilibrium reactions in supine position are appearing and activities in this position are decreasing. Begins to shift to prone position for activities.

Prone position

(ability to lie on stomach)

Developmental sequence: birth

YR. MO.

Birth Cannot raise head for more than a moment. (Labyrinthine righting reaction on head to maintain head in normal position in relation to gravity is absent.) Turns head to side (protective reaction that clears passageway, preventing suffocation). Pelvis is high with knees under abdomen.

0.2 Briefly raises head and demonstrates beginning of labyrinthine righting reaction.

Prone position—cont'd

YR. MO.

0.3 Holds head up 45 to 90 degrees with chest up, hips straight, and knees bent. Weight is on forearms, and propping reaction begins.

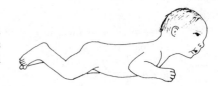

0.5 Props on extended arms.

0.6 Landau response is developing, producing extension of head, spine, and legs when infant is held in ventral suspension. Response is a combination of righting reaction and symmetrical extension; first righting and lifting of head occurs, followed by extension of spine and legs. Equilibrium reactions in prone position are developing.

0.7 Begins more activities in prone position.

0.8 Labyrinthine righting reaction brings head into normal position in space. Propping reaction of arms contributes to lifting upper part of body. Landau response contributes to extending hips. Reciprocal kicking stops, and infant can pivot.

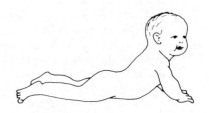

0.9 Total extension and flexor patterns are broken up. Infant can crawl, and symmetrical tonic neck reflex disappears with crawling.

0.10 Creeps.

Roll to side

(ability to roll from back to side lying; involuntary, reflexive)

Developmental sequence: 1-4 weeks

YR. MO.

Birth Sometimes rolls involuntarily from back to side because of curve in his back.

0.3 Earliest reflexive rolling is in response to head being turned and body following, neck righting reaction acting on body. Reaction is strongest at 3 months as asymmetrical tonic neck reflex disappears.

0.4   Vigorously kicks legs so much (reciprocal kicking) that infant may roll to his side. Neck righting is covered up by struggling or other voluntary activity.

Roll prone to supine
(ability to roll from stomach to back; deliberate rolling)

Developmental sequence: 0.6 months

YR. MO.

0.1   Presence of asymmetrical tonic neck
to   reflex is partly responsible for pre-
0.4   venting infant from rolling from prone to supine position and vice versa in early weeks. By 4 months infant assumes symmetrical posture.

0.6   Body-righting-on-body reaction is de-
to   veloping, thus breaking up pattern of
0.8   neck righting (pattern of whole body rolling in response to head turning). When hips or shoulders are turned, other segments follow. Initially, it is from abdominal-lying position to back-lying position. Deliberate rolling is developing.

Roll supine to prone
(ability to roll from back to stomach; deliberate rolling)

Developmental sequence: 0.7 months

YR. MO.

0.7   Rotation of trunk between shoulders and pelvis enables infant to turn over from back-lying position to abdominal-lying position. Initially, infant thrusts his head backward to facilitate rolling. This pattern normally disappears as movement becomes more refined.

Sit up
(ability to attain sitting position)

Developmental sequence: 0.10 months

YR. MO.

Birth   Demonstrates complete head lag when pulled to sitting position. Almost no resistance to gravitational force is evident.

0.2   Considerable head lag is present. Development of labyrinthine righting reaction on head is beginning.

Sit up—cont'd

YR. MO.

0.3   No head lag is present. Lower extremities remain flexed and abducted when infant is pulled to sitting position.

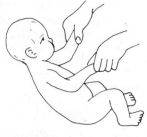

0.5   Lifts head from supine position when about to be pulled up. Some flexion of trunk is evident. Draws lower extremities toward abdomen.

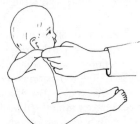

0.6   Lifts head spontaneously from supine position. Optical righting reaction in supine position is developing.

In sitting position head freely rotates without bobbing or plunging. Maintenance of head station is fully developed, effortless, and automatic.

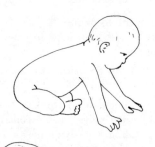

0.10   Attains sitting position with ventral push (change from prone to sitting or sitting to prone).

2.0 to 5.0   Attains sitting position with dorsal push and partial rotation.

5.0   Attains sitting position symmetrically. Body righting (on the body) reaction is integrated.

Propped sitting

(ability to sit with trunk erect, head and chin lifted, with back supported, as in high chair)

Developmental sequence: 0.6 months

YR. MO.

Birth	Back is completely rounded, and head is forward.

0.2	Back is still rounded, and infant raises head well.
0.4	Back is straighter. When infant is held in sitting position, head is held up constantly. Moro reflex is diminishing.

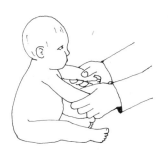

0.5	When infant is held in sitting position, head does not wobble when body is swayed by examiner.
0.6	Sits supported in high chair. Moro reflex is absent.

Sitting/hands props

(ability to sit alone passively without support, hands acting as accessory props)

Developmental sequence: 0.7 months

YR. MO.

Birth	No propping reaction of arms is present.
0.5	Propping reactions are appearing. Hips and knees are flexed (free sitting) when infant is in sitting position.
0.6	Sits with arms forward. Initially hands are fisted but later infant will open hands on supporting surface. Receptive zone of supporting reactions has spread to buttocks, giving back extensor tone.

Sitting/hands props—cont'd
YR. MO.

Parachute reaction (also called *Sprung-bereitschaft* and associated with propping reaction and protective extension of arms) appears whereby arms extend and separate somewhat; fingers extend and spread as if to break fall when infant is suspended horizontally in space, face down, and plunged toward a flat surface.

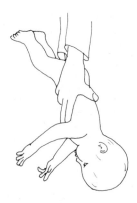

0.7   Sits alone passively without support, and hands act as accessory props.

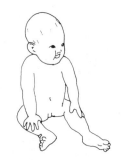

0.8   Sits, using propping reaction of arms sideways. Equilibrium reactions in sitting position are present.

0.9   Can "long sit" with flexed hips and extended legs as total patterns of flexion and extension break up.

0.10   Sits, using propping reaction of arms
to   backward.
1.0

Sitting unsupported
(ability to sit unsupported indefinitely, hands and arms freed for manipulatory duty, eyes elevated)

Developmental sequence: 0.10-0.12 months

YR. MO.

0.8   Sits momentarily on floor without support. Demonstrates protective extension or propping reaction forward and sideways. Moro reflex is absent and startle reaction is fading. (Elbow is flexed and hand is closed in response to strong stimuli such as loud noise.)

Sitting unsupported—cont'd
YR. MO.

0.9   Sits steadily on floor for 10 minutes. Leans forward and recovers balance.

0.10   Sits steadily with little risk of over-balancing. Protective extension backward is developing. Can go over into prone position from sitting or change from prone to sitting position.

1.0   Pivot sitting is present. Can turn to his side within sitting posture, with hands and arms freed for manipulatory duty and eyes elevated. Sits indefinitely when unsupported.

Reaching (maturation progresses from larger muscles of shoulders and upper arm to smaller muscles of wrist, thumb, and index finger)

Reaching to midline
(gross arm movements, developing eye-arm, eye-hand coordination; ability to bring hands together at center of body and grasp object with two-handed approach from supine position)

Developmental sequence: 0.5 months

YR. MO.

Birth   Palmar grasp reflex (tonic reaction of finger flexors) is present. Hands are fisted, thumbs are adducted, and arms are flexed.

Gaze is not yet directed for most objects. Eye reflex responses are present: blinks to sound, movement, or touching of cornea but not to approaching object. Doll's eye response is present (delay in movement of eyes after head is turned in any direction), but response disappears as fixation develops.

0.1.2   Hands are often open, and grasp reflex is reduced.

Eyes can fixate on object, follow moving person, and follow object from side to midline (90 degrees). Does not

Reaching to midline—cont'd

YR. MO.

readily attend to objects less than 9 inches distant, thus his own hands are not visually significant.

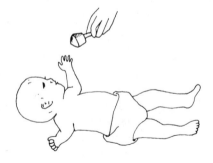

0.2   Hands are frequently open, and grasp reflex is weakening.

Eyes follow person beyond midline and can converge on and focus on objects potentially within his reach, such as his own hand (usually extended hand in preferred tonic neck reflex posture). May fixate on object and make swift swipe with near hand. First object-oriented arm movement occurs, but infant makes no attempt to grasp.

0.3   Hands are loosely open and cannot grasp object without its being placed in hand. Primarily touches object and rarely grasps. Demonstrates sustained hand regard.

Eyes follow 180 degrees. Jerky eruptions of affect occur as a psychomotor expression of joy when object is seen. Fixes eyes well on feeding bottle. Unilateral hand raising occurs (within inch or so of object). Glances repeatedly from object to hand and back. Later unilateral approach decreases in favor of bilateral pattern.

0.4   Frequently brings hands together for clasping. Visual monitoring of their approach and subsequent interplay are usually present and hand regard is still present. Moves arms and legs simultaneously with lively muscle activity. Tries to reach for object but overshoots. Bilateral responses of arms predominate.

Eye-hand coordination begins to develop. Demonstrates immediate regard of dangling object, that is, "grasping with eyes." Can follow object with eyes if object is moved slowly.

Reaching to midline—cont'd

YR. MO.

0.5   Can grasp objects voluntarily and may take them to mouth. Begins visually directed grasping. Uses hand to orient to object and can follow and grasp it. Movements of arms are circumductive, ataxic, and bilateral.

Feet are often elevated.

Binocular vision is established. Must maintain gaze on object or reaching movements are interrupted.

Reaching to mouth and face

(ability to grasp and bring object to mouth or face in sitting position)

Developmental sequence: 0.6 months

YR. MO.

0.6   Holds bottle and brings it to mouth, fingers pressing bottle against palm. Grasp reflex is absent. Sits supported in high chair.

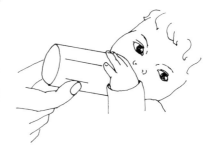

0.7   Feeds self biscuit, using a one-handed approach. Grip is often markedly forced. Transfers object from hand to hand and bangs it on table. Dysmetria in reaching is disappearing. Attention is sustained on object during reaching-prehensile movements.

Reaching to mouth and face—cont'd

YR. MO.

0.10 Reaching for near objects is well-coordinated activity. Sustained attention is no longer demanded because infant can visually appraise before initiating neuromuscular movement. Extension of digits during reach is exaggerated. Voluntary release is beginning.

1.0 Reaching is accomplished by smooth continuous movement with little or no spatial error using a unilateral approach. Digits do not extend until almost in contact with object and then only enough to grasp easily. Has some difficulty releasing small objects.

1.0
to
1.2 Equilibrium reactions in sitting position are developing, permitting functional accomplishment.

Proceed directly to p. 29 (finger foods) for continuation of grasp patterns.

Reaching above head

(ability to reach above head with both arms alternately, maintaining trunk stability when in sitting position)

Developmental sequence: no data

YR. MO.

2.0 Tends to bend at waist and neck and lean forward from buttocks. Can imitate simple movements such as raising arms vertically.

5.0 Functional task of putting on pull-over garment is accomplished.

 Ocular fixation is superior to pursuit.

5.6 Easily loses visual orientation. Experimentally may cross eyes.

6.0 Eyes are better at following.

7.0 Has difficulty in shifting vision from near to far.

8.0 Can shift vision from near to far. In ball throwing, visually loses ball when it comes near.

Reaching behind head

(ability to reach behind head with both arms alternately, maintaining trunk stability, hands together for manipulatory duty when in sitting position)

Developmental sequence: no data

YR. MO.

3.0   Sitting balance is good but awkwardly combined with reaching activity.

4.0   Sitting balance is well maintained. Lacks poise.

5.6   Functional task of closing garment at back (zipper) is accomplished.

6.0   Art of reaching is mastered. Movements of head, trunk, and arms are smoothly synchronized.

Reaching behind back

(ability to reach behind back with both arms alternately, maintaining trunk stability, hands brought together for manipulatory duty)

Developmental sequence: no data

YR. MO.

0.10   Propping reactions of arms backward have developed.

2.0   Reaching results in exaggerated twisting of trunk and marked lateral listing.

3.0   Attempts to cleanse self after toileting but is not very successful.

5.0   Trunk may incline when child is reaching, but head remains erect.

6.0   Can carry out functional task of closing garment at back (tying sash). Cleanses self after toileting.

Reaching to toes

(ability to reach forward with both hands alternately when in sitting position to touch toes, hands free for manipulatory duty; may lean forward on elbows)

Developmental sequence: 1.3 years

YR. MO.

0.8   Adjusts posture to reach object, for example, by leaning forward.

1.0   Equilibrium reactions in sitting position develop.

1.3   Likes to take off shoes.

1.6   When reaching for distant objects, uses opposite hand to support self.

2.0   Reaches for distant object with one hand without supporting self with other.

FEEDING
Swallow liquid
(ability to gather up food and squeeze it to back wall of throat, thereby stimulating swallowing reflex)

Developmental sequence: birth

YR. MO.

Birth   Oral reflexes of rooting, sucking-swallowing, biting, and gagging are present. Negative pressure inside mouth is necessary for efficient sucking. This pressure is created by lips closing round nipple or teat, preventing air coming in instead of liquid, while back of tongue raises to soft palate to close off air coming in from nose. Early awkwardness may be demonstrated by precipitative sucking (tongue cleaving to palate), imperfect approximation of lips with leaking from the corners, or air swallowing. ("Suckling" is first seen, which denotes extension and pulling in pattern of tongue movement as in licking. This is replaced by "sucking" when solids are introduced.)

0.3 to 0.5   Sucking-swallowing and bite reflex are lessening.

0.4   Opens mouth adaptively. Closes lips.

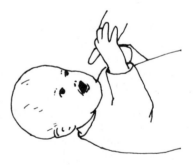

0.6   Takes one or two swallows from a cup. Rooting and sucking-swallowing reflexes are disappearing.

0.7   Chewing is beginning. Gag reflex is weakening (absence of or exaggeration of gag reflex is abnormal at any time).

0.8   Air swallowing is no longer a problem.

0.10   Demonstrates increased tonicity and command of lips, tongue, and jaw.

1.0   Drooling is under control.

2.0   Can suck and use straw and blows with a steady flow of air.

Chew semisolids, solids

(ability to masticate solids by well-defined chewing)

Developmental sequence: 1.6 years

YR. MO.

0.1
to
0.3   Solids may or may not be introduced one at a time. Demonstrates choking response to solids. Tongue thrust is present.

0.4   Gums or mouths solid food. Tongue is used to move food in mouth and projects after spoon is removed. Ejects food with tongue.

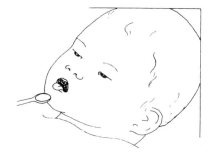

0.5   Is accustomed to solids if they have been introduced early. Bite reflex is diminishing.

0.7   Takes solids well. Chewing is present, and coordination of tongue and pharynx is established.

1.6   Well-defined chewing is demonstrated, and oral patterns are fairly well differentiated and coordinated.

2.0
to
3.0   Chews with mouth closed and shifts food in mouth.

3.0   Uses adult pattern of chewing, which involves rotatory action of jaw.

4.0   Chews and swallows to empty mouth before speaking.

Finger foods

(ability to reach, grasp, and bring finger food to mouth)

Developmental sequence: 0.10 months

YR. MO.

Birth   Grasp reflex, consisting of grip reflex and response to traction, is present. Hand clinches on contact.

0.2   Grasp reflex lessens. Holds object briefly.

0.3   Hand is open, and hand regard occurs.

0.4   Hands are together. Grasp reflex is diminishing, predominantly occurring with last three fingers. Demonstrates hand-to-mouth motions using both hands. Clutches and scratches with hands.

Finger foods—cont'd

YR. MO.

0.5 Grasps voluntarily with palmar grasp and may bring objects to mouth. Ulnar raking with hand present.

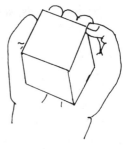

0.6
to
0.7 Feeds self cracker. Grasps with whole hand, using radial approach, and transfers object. Thumb is becoming more useful, and opposition is beginning. Slaps, scratches, and rakes with hands.

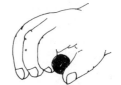

0.8 Demonstrates scissors grasp with thumb pressing object toward index finger. Lateral prehension is present. Approaches objects with index finger. Release is developing.

Demonstrates radial raking.

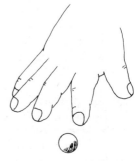

Finger foods—cont'd

YR. MO.

0.10   Feeds self finger foods. Pincer grasp with thumb to index finger is developing, enabling infant to pick up crumbs. Can begin to isolate fingers and demonstrates crude release. Hits, pushes, waves, shakes, and clasps with hands.

0.11   Wrist extension is more obvious when infant is grasping.

1.0   Finger feeds self with small bites of food from plate, using delicate grasp with appropriate amount of force and demonstrating development of release.

2.0 to 6.0   Distinguishes between finger foods and spoon foods.

4.0 to 5.0   Serves self finger foods.

Utensils

(ability to grasp utensil, fill with food, and raise to mouth without spilling)

Bottle

Developmental sequence: 0.10 months

Spoon

Developmental sequence: 3.0 years

YR. MO.

0.6   Anticipates spoon feeding and sucks food from spoon.

1.3   Grasps spoon with pronated forearm. Demonstrates poor filling of spoon and may turn it upside down before it enters mouth.

1.6   Fills spoon but has difficulty in inserting spoon in mouth. Is likely to turn it in mouth and spill considerable amount.

2.0   Inserts spoon in mouth without turning and spills moderate amount.

3.0   Spills small amount from spoon. Girls may have supinated grasp of spoon.

4.0   Holds spoon with fingers when filled with solid foods.

4.0 to 6.0   Holds spoon with fingers when filled with liquid food. Few spills occur.

Cup

Developmental sequence: 1.6 years

YR. MO.

1.3   Holds cup by handle with fingers, but cup is likely to tip. Close supervision is necessary.

1.6   Lifts cup to mouth and drinks well, but may drop cup.

1.9   Handles cup well and lifts, drinks, and replaces it.

Glass

Developmental sequence: 2.0 years

YR. MO.

2.0   Holds small glass in one hand.

Fork

Developmental sequence: 3.0-4.0 years

YR. MO.

2.4   May hold fork in fist.
4.3   Eats with fork held in fingers rather than in fist.
4.6   Chooses fork over spoon when appropriate.

Knife

Developmental sequence: 6.0-8.0 years

YR. MO.

6.0   Spreads with knife.
to
7.0

7.0   Cuts with knife.
to
8.0

TOILETING
Bowel control

(ability to regulate bowels so elimination occurs when seated on toilet)

Developmental sequence: 1.6 years

YR. MO.

1.6   Toilet is regulated.
2.0   Rarely has bowel movement accident.
3.0   Responds to routine times and usually does not have to go to toilet between these.

Bladder control

(ability to maintain sphincter control, remaining dry day and night)

Developmental sequence: 2.0 years

YR. MO.

Birth   Voiding reflex is present, which can be stimulated by handling infant and using other nonspecific stimuli.
0.10   Begins to pay attention to act of voiding. May listen to sound, and general facial expression may reveal his awareness of activity.
1.2   Indicates by gesture or action when he is wet.
to
1.6

1.9   Indicates need to go to toilet.
2.0   Is bladder trained at day time and dry at night if he is taken up.
3.6   Is dry at night if he is not taken up.

Sit on toilet
(ability to climb on lavatory seat unaided)

Developmental sequence: 2.9 years

YR. MO.

1.3	Will sit on toilet when he is placed and supervised (1 minute).
1.5	Will sit on toilet when he is placed and left alone (1 minute).
2.9	Will seat self on toilet.

Arrange clothing
(ability to manage fastenings, to get pants up and down, and to hold dress away from buttocks)

Developmental sequence: 4.0 years

YR. MO.

3.0	Adjusts clothing to go to toilet with assistance.
4.0	Can manage clothes without difficulty.
5.0	Anticipates immediate toilet needs.

Cleanse self

Developmental sequence: 5.0 years

YR. MO.

3.0	Attempts to wipe self but is not very successful.
5.0	Completely cares for self at toilet, including wiping.

Flush toilet

Developmental sequence: 3.3 years

YR. MO.

5.0	Flushes toilet after each use.

HYGIENE
Turn faucets on/off

Developmental sequence: 3.0-4.0 years

Wash and dry hands/face
(ability to wash and dry hands and face efficiently unsupervised without a reminder of technique)

Developmental sequence: 4.9 years

YR. MO.

3.6	Dries hands without supervision.
3.9	Washes hands without supervision. Poor wrist rotation of boys may be observed in hand washing when they cannot do customary rotatory movement but instead rub two palmar sufaces together.
4.0	Disposes of paper towel into waste basket. Replaces towel on accessible rack.
4.9	Washes face without supervision.
6.0	Washes hands at appropriate times, such as before meals, after toileting, and when dirty.

Wash ears

Developmental sequence: 8.0-9.0 years

Bathing
(ability to care for all needs when bathing)

Developmental sequence: 8.0 years

YR. MO.

4.0	Dries self with supervision.
	Washes self with supervision.
4.6	Soaps cloth and washes self independently.
5.0	Dries self independently.
7.6	Prepares water for tub or shower.
8.0	Bathes (cares for all needs) when he is reminded to bathe or shower.
9.0	Bathes or showers routinely without suggestion.

Deodorant

Developmental sequence: 12.0- years

YR. MO.

12.0-	Uses a deodorant daily.

Care for teeth
(ability to combine all operations, that is, prepares, brushes, and rinses)

Developmental sequence: 4.9 years

YR. MO.

3.0	Uses brushing motion on tooth surfaces with adult supervision.
3.6	Wets brush and applies toothpaste.
4.9	Combines all operations, that is, prepares, brushes, and rinses.
7.0	Brushes teeth after meals or at routine time.

Care for nose
(ability to blow nose without assistance)

Developmental sequence: 6.0 years

YR. MO.

3.0	Wipes nose with tissue with adult direction.
3.6	Indicates by gesture an awareness of runny nose.
	Requests a tissue to wipe nose.
4.6	Attempts to blow nose when requested.
6.0	Blows nose without assistance.

Care for hair
(ability to comb or brush hair using mirror to check style)

Developmental sequence: 7.6 years

YR. MO.

4.0	Attempts to comb hair.
5.0	Combs hair with supervision.
6.6	Brushes hair free of all tangles.
7.6	Combs hair using mirror to check style.
12.0	Uses rollers to set hair (girls).
	Uses hair spray to hold combed style.

Care for nails
(ability to scrub or file nails)

Developmental sequence: 8.0 years

YR. MO.

5.6   Scrubs fingernails with brush.
8.0   Maintains clean nails.
      Files nails.
      Clips nails on both hands.
      Cuts toenails.

Feminine hygiene

Developmental sequence: puberty

UNDRESSING
LOWER BODY
Untie shoe bow

Developmental sequence: 2.0-3.0 years

Remove shoes
(ability to untie shoe bow and remove shoes)

Developmental sequence: 2.0-3.0 years

YR. MO.
1.3   Likes to take off shoe.
2.0   Removes shoe if lace is untied.

Remove socks

Developmental sequence: 1.6 years

Remove pull-down garment (shorts, panties, pants)

Developmental sequence: 2.6 years

YR. MO.
2.0   Helps to push down garments.
2.6   Removes pull-down garments that have elastic waist.
3.0   Is independent with pull-down garment.

UPPER BODY
Remove pull-over garment (T-shirt, sweater, dress)

Developmental sequence: 4.0 years

YR. MO.
3.0   Assistance is needed.
4.0   Little assistance is required.

DRESSING
LOWER BODY
Put on socks

Developmental sequence: 4.0 years

YR. MO.

3.0   Has difficulty in turning heel.
4.0   Little assistance is required.

Put on pull-down garment (shorts, panties, pants)
(ability to put on garment, right side out, with
front and back correctly placed)

Developmental sequence: 4.0 years

YR. MO.

3.0   Does not know front from back.
4.0   Little assistance is needed and can turn clothing right side out.
5.0   Dresses with care.

Girls dress themselves more efficiently and earlier than boys because of a better fine motor coordination and especially a more flexible wrist rotation.

Put on shoe
(ability to put shoe on correct foot)

Developmental sequence: 4.0 years

YR. MO.

0.11   Holds foot out for shoe.
1.6   Tries to put on shoe.
3.0   Puts on shoe, but it may be on wrong foot.
4.0   Little assistance is needed.

Lace shoe

Developmental sequence: 4.0 years

YR. MO.

3.0   Tries to lace, usually incorrectly.
4.0   Laces shoe with some difficulty; later laces shoe with ease.

Tie bow

Developmental sequence: 6.0 years

YR. MO.

5.3   Ties knot (overhand).
6.0   Ties bowknot.

UPPER BODY
Put on pull-over garment (T-shirt, dress, sweater)

Developmental sequence: 5.0 years

YR. MO.

0.11   Holds arm out for sleeve.
2.0   Finds large arm hole.

Put on pull-over garment—cont'd
YR. MO.

3.0	May need assistance.
4.0	Distinguishes front and back and puts garment on correctly. Turns clothing right side out.
5.0	Dresses with care.

FASTENERS—unfastening
Button
YR. MO.

3.0	Opens front and side buttons.
5.6	Opens back buttons.

Zipper
YR. MO.

3.3	Opens front zipper on pants or jacket.
3.6	Opens separating front zipper on jacket.
4.9	Opens back zipper.

Buckle
YR. MO.

3.9	Unbuckles belt or shoe.

Tie
YR. MO.

5.0	Unties back sash on apron or dress.

FASTENERS—fastening
Button
YR. MO.

2.6	Buttons one large front button.
3.6	Buttons series of three buttons.
6.3	Buttons back buttons.

Zipper
YR. MO.

4.0	Closes front zipper and locks tab.
4.6	Closes separating zipper.
5.6	Closes back zipper.

Buckle
YR. MO.

4.0	Buckles belt or shoes.
4.6	Inserts belt in loops.

Tie

YR. MO.

6.0　　Ties apron or dress sash in front.
8.0　　Ties apron or dress sash in back.
10.0　　Ties necktie.

Snaps

YR. MO.

3.0　　Closes front snaps.
6.0　　Snaps back snaps.

REFERENCES

Blockley, J., and Miller, G. 1971. Feeding techniques with cerebral-palsied children. Physiotherapy 57:300-307.

Bobath, K. 1966. The motor deficit in patients with cerebral palsy. Spastics International Medical Publications in association with William Heinemann Medical Books, Ltd.

Comprehensive Coordinated Curriculum, Special Education Department Monterey County Office of Education, Monterey Pupil Developmental Progress Scale, Salinas, Calif.

Fiorentino, M. R. 1974. Reflex testing methods for evaluating C.N.S. development, ed. 2. Springfield, Charles C Thomas, Publisher.

Gesell, A. 1940. The first five years of life—a guide to the study of the pre-school child. New York, Harper & Row, Publishers.

Illingworth, R. S. 1966. The development of the infant and young child—normal and abnormal, ed. 3. Baltimore, The Williams & Wilkins Co.

Knoblock, H., and Pasamanick, B. 1974. Arnold Gesell and Catherine Amatruda's developmental diagnosis, ed. 3. New York, Harper & Row, Publishers.

Knopp, C. editor. 1971. Readings in early development. Springfield, Ill., Charles C Thomas, Publisher.

Marlow, D. R. 1969. Textbook of pediatric nursing. Philadelphia, W. B. Saunders Co.

McGraw, M. B. 1943. The neuromuscular maturation of the human infant. New York, Columbia University Press.

Pearson, P., and Williams, C. A., editors. 1972. Physical therapy services in the developmental disabilities. Springfield, Ill., Charles C Thomas, Publisher.

Peiper, A. 1963. Cerebral function in infancy and childhood. New York, Consultants Bureau Enterprises, Inc.

5 *Neuromotor maturation and self-care development*

The process by which a child acquires the skill to function independently in his daily activities has been presented in outline form so that each sequence of development can be seen more distinctly. It is equally important that the reader be able to synthesize the material into a composite and conceptualize the process as a whole.

THE NEWBORN

The newborn comes into the world with little voluntary, controlled movement at his disposal. Occasionally his movement is self-initiated, but more often it is reflexive or a response to sensory stimuli. His muscle tone is dominated by flexor patterns, and motor responses are total and nonspecific. The reflex mechanism provided by nature assists him to survive, but externally he requires persons to protect and nourish him during the time when voluntary patterns of movement are emerging.

Consider the extent of his initial helplessness and dependency. He has no ability to adjust to the forces of gravity. He cannot raise his head for more than a moment but can turn it to the side when prone, thus clearing the passageway and preventing suffocation (Peiper, 1963). If he rolls to the side, it is an involuntary action that may be due to the curve in his back or a reflexive response to having his head turned. If his hand grips an extended finger placed in his palm, it is a tonic reaction of his own finger flexors, not a purposeful motor expression. His gaze is not directed, unless visual objects are within a particular range of sensory values, and eye responses are largely a reflexive reaction to stimuli. Sucking and swallowing, which appear so vigorous and self-initiated, are under reflexive control. Voiding can be stimulated by someone picking him up or moving him about, and this too is an automatic involuntary response to stimuli.

The primitive reflexes that are present at birth and have just been described include the palmar grasp, neck righting, voiding, and oral reflexes of rooting, sucking-swallowing, and biting. There are others as well, but since an individual can potentially attain independence with aids, such as a "sitting person," attention is directed here to reflexes that influence function described in this handbook and those self-care activities most closely associated with occupational therapy. Neuromotor requirements for standing and walking therefore are not included.

PRIMITIVE REFLEXES THAT EMERGE AFTER BIRTH

Other primitive reflexes may be noted after the first month, such as the asymmetrical and symmetrical tonic neck reflexes. These primitive reflexes do more than assist the baby to survive; they provide movement and control posture tone, but they do not produce static unyielding positions in the normal infant. They are intermittent postures, amidst spontaneous motor activity, which influence movement without controlling it. At the same time reflexes modify one another. In the plan of reflex mechanism, reflexes are dependent on one another and build on one another (Ford, 1975).

HOW REFLEXES AFFECT MOTOR FUNCTION

It is fascinating to study the correlation between the inhibition and integration of neonatal automatic responses to stimuli and the emergence of more voluntary control. This relationship has been described by Bobath (1966) and others, and evidence is contained in Chapter 4; for example, the influence of oral reflexes on the feeding patterns of the infant can be noted. At birth he possesses a rooting reflex. With stimulation to the area around the mouth, the tongue moves toward the stimulus and the head turns to follow. This assists the infant in locating the source of his food (Illingworth, 1966). By 6 months of age, after the reflex disappears, the infant is ready to take one or two swallows from a cup. He no longer needs the assistance of a reflex in searching out sustenance.

Similarly, the newborn shows a biting reflex. When the lower gum is stimulated, his jaw opens and closes with up-and-down movements. Before a baby can acquire more advanced rotatory movements of the jaw, the bite reflex must be inhibited. Fading of the reflex begins during the third to fifth months and the reflex disappears completely by the seventh month when the chewing reflex begins. Discrete rotatory movements of the jaw characteristic of a mature pattern will not be seen until about the third year (Finnie, 1970).

The Moro reflex is present at birth and is demonstrated by a strong abductor-extensor reaction of various parts of the body with loss of support that results in shaking of the head. This reflex fades and is integrated by 6 months, when the baby begins to sit erect in a high chair and utilize propping reactions of his arms (Bobath, 1966). The startle reaction remains but with diminution. Otherwise the baby would be unable to maintain sitting stability in the presence of stimuli.

The asymmetrical tonic neck reflex appears after the first month and influences, but does not control, the position of the extremities in relation to the position of the head. When the head is turned to the side, face limbs may extend, and the skull limbs flex with postural tone increasing. Ford (1975) states that the baby "can willfully move his limbs into other positions but he is inclined to assume the asymmetrical posture, which is useful for it permits the infant freedom to turn his head without rolling his body."[*] When this reflex fades at 4 months, one also notes that the baby

*From Ford, F., 1975. Normal motor development in infancy. In Bleck, E. E., and Nagel, D. A., editors: Physically handicapped children—a medical atlas for teachers, p. 165. New York, Grune & Stratton, Inc. By permission.

frequently clasps his hands together, a feat made easier with symmetrical posture. Likewise, he is in a better anatomical position to master the task of rolling, which he begins to practice from the prone position at 6 months.

This is not to say that the baby does not roll over before 6 months. Researchers know that he responds to stimuli through receptors in the neck and labyrinth of the ear so that when his head is turned, he rolls over as a unit. This is the neck righting reaction acting on the body. It is also characteristic for a baby to kick vigorously at this age, a behavior that has been labeled "reciprocal kicking." At 4 months of age he may kick with such enthusiasm while supine that he rolls to his side, and the neck righting reflex is then covered up by the struggling of other voluntary activity. At 6 months a new "reaction" emerges that profoundly affects the process of rolling. This reaction, called "body righting" (on the body), breaks up the neck righting pattern and enables the baby to rotate within his body axis. First his shoulders turn, then the hips, or vice versa. The turning can be done segmentally rather than the body turning as a whole (Bobath, 1966), and thus "log rolling" is replaced. Given the neurological possibility of segmental turning, the baby begins to practice first from the prone position, then the supine position, until he masters his skill to roll deliberately.

Reciprocal kicking is a motor behavior that is often combined with heightened excitement and animation and is delightful to watch. It is, however, a transitory phase and disappears around the eighth month (Bobath, 1966; Illingworth, 1966), when the infant begins to show a preference for the prone position. Kicking is replaced by extension of the legs and back, and the infant practices pivoting on his stomach.

Although little attention has been devoted to the symmetrical tonic neck reflex in this handbook, its influence should not be overlooked. The reflex occurs when there is sufficient stimulation of proprioceptors of the neck muscles with some contribution from joint receptors. Thus, when the head is flexed, the arms flex and the legs extend; when the head is extended, the arms extend and legs flex. Some authorities credit the midline position of the head and symmetrical posture in the 4-month-old baby with the influence of the symmetrical tonic neck reflex over the asymmetrical tonic neck reflex (Sukiennicki, 1971).

Until the symmetrical tonic neck reflex fades, however, it is difficult for a baby to assume and maintain a quadruped position on hands and knees for creeping. With movements of his head into flexion or extension, either arms or legs may collapse into flexion. Indeed, as noted, the reflex disappears around the eighth month before creeping on hands and knees begins and propping reactions are steady.

OTHER PATTERNS OF DEVELOPMENT THAT INFLUENCE
MOTOR FUNCTION

The development of voluntary control is aided by other patterns in addition to the inhibition of primitive reflexes. In the illustrations in Chapter 4 it can be seen that total flexion and extension gradually subside over the first 10 months of life. One indication of this occurring is when the baby, lying supine with extended arms, can grasp his feet and bring them flexed to his mouth, which occurs around 6 months of age. A further indication of the influence of these total patterns can be seen when the child first sits. Initially, both hips and knees flex, a characteristic that assessors label "free" sitting. At 9 months of age the infant sits with hips flexed and knees extended, a posture called "long" sitting. This signifies that the total patterns of flexion and extension are broken up (Bobath, 1966) and that the infant has more variety in the positions he can assume.

Another pattern to observe in a baby's development is the change in his preferred position. He comes into the world from the uterus where he developed from an embryo, curled within the unique environment of the amniotic sac. His muscle tone, as noted previously, is strongly dominated by the physiological hypertonus of flexion. Over the first few months of life, this flexor tone begins to lessen, first in the upper extremities, then in the lower. As this happens, one can follow the progress by observing the profile of the baby lying prone. At birth the pelvis is high because of the flexor tone of the hips and knees (Illingworth, 1966). By the sixth month the pelvis is not only flat because of the relaxation of flexor tone but the development of tone is increasing in the direction of extension, which prepares the baby for sitting and standing. This can be seen in the Landau response at 6 months of age, whereby when the baby is held suspended, his head and back arch with the concavity upward (Bobath, 1966). There is also partial extension of the lower limbs at the hip joints. By the seventh month the baby is beginning more activities in the prone position with extension posture, and activities in the supine position decrease.

DIRECTION OF DEVELOPMENT

There is direction to development from head to foot, proximally to distally and medially to laterally. Before he walks, the baby first learns to control his head and later explores his environment with his hands, manipulating objects.

The development of "reach" illustrates the proximal to distal direction. For example, at about 2 months of age the baby makes swiping movements of his arms from the shoulders but makes no attempt to grasp objects, since the hands are typically fisted (White, Castle, and Held, 1971). He continues stretching, overshooting, and circumducting his arms in space. It is not until about the fifth month that the baby can voluntarily reach for and prehend objects with his hands, often bringing them to his mouth.

The development of grasp further shows the medial-to-lateral direction. A baby voluntarily grasps with his whole hand at 5 to 6 months of age. On occasions he reaches out and rakes objects, using the fingers and palm ulnarly. As he practices grasping objects over and over, his prehension shifts radially, with his thumb becoming more useful. Finally, the thumb presses objects toward the index finger, and lateral prehension is present at about the eighth month.

LEARNING TO COPE WITH GRAVITY

As the child develops his moving and exploring abilities, he is helped by "reactions" closely associated with normal postural tone. They allow him to maintain his posture against gravity and gradually free his extremities for tasks other than balancing. With the help of these equilibrium reactions he is free to manipulate and experiment with objects and to touch shapes, textures, and sizes that exist in his environment. At the same time reflexes that will be present for life emerge to assist him in the orientation of his head in space and in the proper alignment of the head and neck with the trunk and of the trunk with the limbs (Bobath, 1966).

The labyrinthine righting reaction is absent at birth. Evidence of its development is seen in the second month as the baby raises his head briefly from the prone position (Peiper, 1963). Each month as he grows stronger, he lifts his head progressively higher, and by the eighth month the reaction brings the head into normal position in space.

The labyrinthine righting reaction develops a little later in the supine position and coincides with the appearance of the optical righting reflex. The optical righting reflex is of secondary importance initially but gains quickly in influence as the child grows. Mysak (1968) states, "The head follows movements of the eyes and hence the eyes contribute to head orientation."* Initially, the baby has complete head lag when pulled to sitting. By 6 months he can lift his head spontaneously and, when placed in a high chair, maintains head station effortlessly and automatically, without bobbing or plunging (Gesell, 1940).

Propping reactions of the arms assist the baby in becoming a sitting person and the first sign of their development occurs as the infant lies prone at 2 to 3 months of age, bearing weight on his forearms (Peiper, 1963). At 6 months when sitting, he uses his hands as props to maintain balance and places them forward when sitting. If he tilts sideways or backward, he topples over. By 7 months he is moving his arms closer to his sides and opposite his trunk for balancing, and by 10 months he utilizes propping reactions backward (Bobath, 1966).

At the same time that the baby starts to use propping reactions of his arms, he begins to acquire equilibrium reactions, but the pace differs significantly (Bobath, 1966). For example, equilibrium in the prone and supine positions develops at 6 and 7 months of age when the baby is already sitting; equilibrium develops in the sitting position subsequent to the time when he is creeping. It is not fully developed in standing until the second year, some time after he takes his first steps.

CONCLUSION

We have seen how the newborn profits from the primitive reflex mechanisms. They assist him to survive and provide automatic movement that he can practice. With the fading of primitive reflexes, he is in a position to modify movement and achieve more voluntary control. Progressing from a supine and prone environment, he comes to grips with the forces of gravity and is helped through "reactions" that allow for the maintenance of position in space and the performance of normal move-

---

*From Mysak, E. D.: Neuroevolutional approach to cerebral palsy and speech, p. 18. New York, Copyright 1968 by Teachers College, Columbia University.

ment. Finally, as a sitting and standing individual with fine manipulatory skill, he is physiologically equipped to carry out activities of daily living independently.

REFERENCES

Bobath, K. 1966. The motor deficit in patients with cerebral palsy. Spastics International Medical Publications in association with William Heinemann Medical Books, Ltd.

Finnie, N. 1970. Handling the cerebral palsied child at home. New York. E. P. Dutton & Co., Inc.

Ford, F. 1975. Normal motor development in infancy. In Bleck, E. E., and Nagel, D. A., editors: Physically handicapped children—a medical atlas for teachers. New York, Grune & Stratton, Inc.

Gesell, A. 1940. The first five years of life—a guide to the study of the pre-school child. New York, Harper & Row, Publishers.

Illingworth, R. S. 1966. The development of the infant and young child—normal and abnormal, ed. 3. Baltimore, The Williams & Wilkins Co.

Mysak, E. D. 1968. Neuroevolutional approach to cerebral palsy and speech. New York, Teachers College Press.

Peiper, A. 1963. Cerebral function in infancy and childhood. New York, Consultants Bureau Enterprises, Inc.

Sukiennicki, D. A.: Neuromotor development. In Banus, B. S.: The developmental therapist. Thorofare, N.J., 1971, Charles B. Slack, Inc.

White, B. L., Castle, P., and Held, R. 1971. Observations on the development of visually directed reaching. In Knopp, C., editor: Readings in early development. Springfield, Ill., Charles C Thomas, Publisher.

6 *Other behavioral components in developing independence for self-care tasks*

Independence is more than motoric expression. The act of voluntarily performing undirected functional tasks requires not only physical, perceptual motor, and cognitive skill but also constitutional drives and certain concepts of one's self. The all-encompassing process that prepares one for independence and, later, maintains the state of self-sufficiency starts at birth and lasts throughout life.

One of the major tasks for the infant is to detach himself from his mother and gain autonomy. He is aided in this task by his increased competency in motor skills, particularly locomotion. He begins to acquire speech as well as nonverbal ways of relating to people in his environment and becomes increasingly aware of their attitudes toward him. Through myriad experiences of childhood he slowly develops a concept of self and later, in adolescence, a sense of identity. Ultimately, to cope with the responsibility of self-care tasks and to achieve emotional and economic independence satisfactorily, he must have acquired prerequisite traits of initiative, self-reliance, industry, satisfaction in accomplishment, and skills leading to confidence in his ability to be self-sufficient. Such fortitudes provide the motivation and drive that allow him to free himself from the security of dependence. Independence is not an absolute state once achieved, however. It is an ongoing process that can fluctuate with stress and individual needs for support at any one time. A consideration of forces influencing growth in independence provides perspective in understanding this more complicated, internal process.

THE NEWBORN

The extent of the newborn's helplessness and his dependency on others for protection, comfort, and nurture were noted earlier. In the months following birth the baby cries out when he seeks relief from physiological discomfort. Needs are expressed instinctually in a normally demanding way. However, Senn and Solnit (1968) believe that even the newborn has his own particular and primary way of reacting—

45

his own "personality," so to speak; and Brazelton (1969) emphasizes that babies possess strong, inborn differences that predetermine particular styles of development. Others cite the mother's condition during pregnancy and in the period after birth as probable influences on the newborn's personality.

Studies by Gesell (1940) over thirty years ago indicated that at 1 month of age a baby might momentarily regard a face leaning over him, but according to Gesell, this fleeting contact was the extent of his social ability. Presently, authorities acknowledge more signs of responsiveness to social stimuli during the neonatal period (Brazelton, 1969). Various investigators have measured visual attentiveness in the newborn and some believe, on the basis of their comprehensive examinations of early sensory systems, that about half of the babies who are awake fixate and track a presented target centrally. Cohen and Salapatek (1975) edited two volumes that discuss studies of infant perception, from the techniques and methods used in measuring infant vision to a variety of existing theories of perceptual development.

MOTHER-CHILD RELATIONSHIP

Initially, then, the infant's world centers around himself. It is believed that he is unable to differentiate himself from human and nonhuman environment; body and surroundings are continuous (Spitz, 1965). He does not distinguish himself from objects nor from other persons, including his mother, or mothering figure, his chief source of physiological gratification.

It is in the close mother-child relationship that expectations and attitudes begin to play a part in the development of independence. As the mother satisfies the infant's physiological needs, he comes to trust and recognize the consistency of her maternal care and her ability to relieve discomfort (Erikson, 1963). During the nurturing process both positive and negative feelings are communicated frequently and repetitiously by touch, voice tone, and other stimulation. The mother becomes the all-important love object as the infant begins to want her love and praise.

This first relationship, deeply significant in developmental influence, undergoes changes as the child matures and requires adjustments to interaction. This can be illustrated by observing the consequences of the infant's increasing motor competency. As he acquires more control, he can expand his area of exploration. With balance established, he reaches out and touches objects, mouths them, drops them, and finally throws them. He has a compulsion to be active, to move and gain mastery of his body (Fraiberg, 1959).

For her part the mother must now provide more than comforting and nurturing. She must limit the child in his impetuous exploration, both to protect him as well as to preserve the environment. She also comes to expect certain performances from him that reflect the standards in her own upbringing and also the standards current in the cultural group. Vander Veer (1949) explains that the process is one of continuous conflict between the child's basic impulses and the socially imposed standards:

"In this struggle, the child's allegiance is divided. On the one hand, he wants to retain his impulses in their unchanged form, and, on the other hand, he wishes to retain his mother's love by the requirements which she sets for him."*

Kent (1971) points out that prior to the development of language, it is difficult for the child to forego these behaviors because his instinctual needs to explore and manipulate far outweigh his capacity to control. With the development of language, words come to substitute for the act or object. Luria (1960) speaks to this point as well. Verbal expression provides an alternative, and the experience of using words helps the child to gain control over his impulsive behaviors.

Most significantly, the child gradually absorbs his mother's standards into his conscience, his superego, which then acts as an internal force to prohibit the primitive expression of his physiological and emotional drives. Vander Veer further explains that the drives which have been brought under control, in their turn, are allowed to find more socially acceptable forms of expression in line with what the mother will permit. "If one of mother's requirements is self-sufficiency, she allows the child to gradually wean himself from his dependency on her, in this way helping him to become physically and psychologically independent."*

RELATIONSHIPS WITH OTHERS

As the child detaches himself from the mother, he also enlarges his social interactions with others. Gillette (1971) notes that this interaction occurs primarily among family figures at first and later expands to include peer groups and others in the community. This, too, is a gradual process involving conceptual development and sublimation of impulses. Initially, he encounters playmates physically, but social contacts are brief. He may hug or push peers out of the way as though they are physical objects (Gesell and Ilg, 1943). For the most part his play is solitary, or he may periodically look on at the activity around him. Later he may be within the group physically, playing alongside others but engrossed in his own activity. Hesitantly, he begins to share toys and his interest is heightened through entering into tasks that require combined effort, as in block play. Dramatization awakens imaginative powers, furnishes increased social awareness and interaction with playmates, and provides practice in distinguishing roles in the world about him. Simple fundamental principles necessary in social groups, such as waiting turns and taking responsibility for restoring order to the play area, prepare him for the adaptive skills he will need in adjusting to the school experience.

School is a structured environment for the grouping that occurs at this age and

---

*From Vander Veer, A. H.: Occupational therapy in a children's hospital—a psychiatric viewpoint. Presented before the Tri-State Hospital Assembly, Palmer House, Chicago, May 2, 1949. The late Dr. Vander Veer had been Associate Professor of Psychiatry, University of Chicago Medical School, and Director of the Service in Child Psychiatry at the University Clinics and the Bobs Roberts Memorial Hospital for Children, Chicago, Ill.

the ensuing competition and rivalry. It is an extended period devoted to mastery of skills. Academic skill building proceeds according to an orderly plan, and through spontaneous play the child develops physical prowess. Now he easily runs, jumps, hops, climbs, throws, and catches. Refinement occupies his attention, and repetition of feats leads to modification in his coordination and finer precision of movement. Both skills and games become increasingly complex while at the same time requiring more sophisticated levels of cooperation, adherence to rules, and contribution of joint effort.

Kent (1971) points out that much of the play of childhood occurs outside of organized activities through gangs formed by children themselves. Membership is not necessarily specified but is understood through the amount of approval won from within the group. Both positive and negative social behaviors may be exhibited, and there is strong pressure toward conformity with the majority decision.

The desire for peer approval continues to grow in the period of adolescence. Physiological changes of puberty in effect alter relationships, and the adolescent draws away from adults in his attempt to find a role as a mature male or female figure. Kent explains that the family remains important as the source of support and identification but not as the source of sexual expression.

The adolescent's struggle for independence, coupled with his limited experiences, can be a source of stress both for him and those adults attempting to provide guidance. He may at times surge toward an independent status for himself that is either in reality beyond his capacity or, in his more introspective moments, seemingly beyond his capacity. This has the effect of frightening him, more commonly at a subconscious level. Josselyn (1960) believes that at such times the adult becomes the stabilizer by allowing the adolescent to be dependent until he again mobilizes his internal strength sufficiently to pursue independence. Out of this vacillation between independence and dependence, some type of cohesiveness finally emerges.

INDUSTRY

Interpersonal relationships play an essential part in the child's evolving sense of self. The attitudes of others toward him influence his view of his strengths and weaknesses and his sense of self-esteem. These reactions and responses occur within an environment of activity in school, work, and play.

The use of tools serves to illustrate the dynamics. Initially, gratification comes through manipulation and experimentation with tools and materials. The satisfaction lies, in great part, with the process itself and the visual, tactile, and kinesthetic sensations that result from activity. As peers and adults react to the child's efforts and focus on his finished product, his psyche absorbs the attitudinal content and causes him to form judgments about his own adequacy. Kent (1971) states that he believes he must earn the love and esteem of others by producing things, and with repetition he comes to feel gratification at a job well done. The psychological result of production, in turn, affects his motivation and drive toward industry.

Industry also involves building habits for work and self-discipline. With increased maturity the child learns to put work ahead of play in appropriate situations. He begins to organize his time and energy to get a piece of work done. The performance of chores around the house is helpful in developing responsibility. Later, in adolescence, work experience is important in further defining responsibility, providing a basis for occupational choice and giving him some measure of assurance that he has the capacity for economic independence.

SELF-CARE REVIEW

We have traced the process of detachment from the mother, the development of self-image, the capacity to relate to others, and the social adaptation in cooperative tasks. The importance of industry has been described as a precursor to economic independence by setting up attitudes of satisfaction from accomplishment and by establishing basic habits of work. As an adolescent, the individual faces the major developmental tasks of securing identity and further appraising his basic strengths and weaknesses on a realistic basis. Finally, he approaches the zenith step of moving from his home, out into the world.

Against this background a scanning study of Chapter 4 has deeper dimensions. Development occurs through transition and follows a wavering course. Maturational changes are not sudden and abrupt but gradual and overlapping. Distortion of the spiraling process tends to occur when "development" is translated into narrative form. Nonetheless, viewing it chronologically assists in organizing and visualizing its many facets.

Fourth month

Hand facility is a major requirement in performing self-care tasks. The ability to bring the hands together at 4 months is thus a significant milestone. It is also an appealing posture, made more so with the newly acquired vocalizations of cooing, gurgling, and laughter. The infant can follow with his eyes, and, if bottle-fed, will open his mouth adaptively when a bottle is presented. The mother, or mother figure, is recognized through numerous, patterned expectancies of care.

Tenth month

By 10 months of age the infant is fairly well established in routines of everyday life (Gesell, 1940). He sleeps through the night, takes solids well, holds his own bottle, and can feed himself finger foods with a pincer grasp. He is often fascinated by his own adeptness in picking up crumbs.

Sitting posture has become steady so that when the infant is placed on the floor or in his playpen, there is little risk of overbalancing. With agility he goes over into the prone position from sitting or changes from prone to sitting. Manipulatory skills are developing rapidly, and in his play with toys he practices grasp and release, which are crude movements. He enjoys shaking objects as well as hitting and waving them. Thus he is self-contained for periods of time, but when strangers approach, he exhibits a distress reaction. Anxiously he freezes in postural stance, and his mouth begins to pucker because he is learning to differentiate the human face and experiences unfamiliarity.

This period has been described as one of "stranger anxiety." Spitz (1965) believes that as the infant establishes the mother as his love object, a stranger's face suggests that he has lost her, and thus he reacts timidly, on occasion with fear, punctuated by cries and screams.

First year

By 1 year of age the child is frequently a focus for family group interaction. He begins to acquire speech, and interest in his vocabulary is a topic among family members. Much of his emotional expression is highly egocentric because he makes a meager distinction between himself and others.

Second year

At 2 years of age the child still has a fragmentary sense of self, but with locomotion he has the physical means to begin detaching himself from his mother. Moreover, he can let her out of his sight because he can carry an image of her through his emerging perceptual skill of form constancy and through memory. He is decidedly motor minded, and his most numerous and characteristic satisfactions are motor (Gesell, 1940). He takes an interest in assisting with dressing and undressing activity, finding armholes in his garments, and noting fastenings. Toilet training is introduced with inconsistent results until he yields to the desire to please his parents. Independence in feeding has progressed to a point where he uses a spoon with only moderate spilling, and he even manages a fork clumsily with his fist. He handles a cup well.

Third year

The 3-year-old is adapting to basic requirements for self-sufficiency. He feeds himself with little spilling, rarely needing assistance to complete a meal. He shows even greater interest in dressing but has more ability in undressing, such as in removing a pull-down garment. He attends to one task at a time, and when he is concentrating on dressing, talking ceases. Perceptually, dressing is a challenge to him. He does not know front from back, and he has difficulty turning the heel of his sock. He tries to put on his shoe, but it may be on the wrong foot. He even attempts lacing but usually incorrectly. Part of his persistence may be because of his increased interest in finer manipulations, including play material. He now occupies himself in sedentary play for longer periods, but massive muscles are still dominant and require interludes for expansive play. His adventures in independence are unpredictable and brief, and the comfort of parental protection draws him back to adults.

Fourth year

The 4-year-old responds to accomplishment. Now he independently manages clothing for toileting and washes both hands and face unsupervised; bathing is an easy routine. He requires little assistance with dressing, can turn clothing right side out, and distinguish front and back correctly. He manages buttons in a series, closes a front zipper, locking the tab, and buckles a belt or shoes. Lacing is still an effort, but progress is steady.

Socially, the 4-year-old prefers playmates to solitary play, and his imagination is lively. Through dramatic play he strives to identify himself with his culture and to understand its intricacies. He is also full of questions and takes pleasure in listening to explanations.

Motor drive is still strong, and skill is coming under finer control. In eating he holds both spoon and fork with his fingers rather than a fist, and a supinated grasp may be seen in the plate-to-mouth pattern. Awkwardly, he begins to attempt to comb his hair.

Sitting balance is well maintained, if somewhat lacking in poise, and he sits for longer periods engaging in interesting manual tasks. Now he can work and talk at the same time.

Fifth year

The 5-year-old is ready for enlarged community experience and is prepared to be sufficient in most self-care tasks. He can anticipate immediate toilet needs and completely care for himself at the toilet, including wiping and flushing the toilet after each use. His skill in using tools enables him to combine all operations of caring for his teeth, including preparing, brushing, and rinsing. He combs his hair with supervision and scrubs fingernails with a brush when coached to do so. All dressing is done with care. He can tie an overhand knot but may not be able to integrate the more advanced perceptual motor task of tying a bow.

Sixth year

The 6-year-old puts finishing touches to the self-care tasks of early childhood. He masters bow tying, and when reaching, his body adjusts to forces of gravity with movements of the head, trunk, and arms smoothly synchronized. Thus he can close garments in the back. His skill in using a knife is improving but primarily for spreading rather than cutting. He assumes responsibility for washing his hands at appropriate times. He can even blow his nose without assistance and, if not feeling too impatient, may persist and brush his hair free of tangles.

Six is a transition age in that society now introduces more formally the tools and elements of its culture. But according to Gesell and Ilg (1943), to understand the more abstract mental material, he requires rich experience with things through handicraft and group activities so that he may make a sound development of words, ideas, and attitudes.

Later childhood

The first 6 years of life represent the formative period, the time span when the most basic patterns are established. Mastery and refinement follow.

New self-care tasks now occur gradually and naturally in the remaining years of childhood. For example, the child begins to prepare his own water for tub or shower, and in time he will take care of all bathing routinely without direction; likewise, brushing the teeth becomes routine. Combing the hair may involve developing a style, with some mediation between parental and peer-group preferences. The task of filing nails requires more intricate motor planning and takes practice but is gradually mastered. Depending on the cultural group, a boy may undergo instruction in how to tie a necktie.

Adolescence

Puberty presents a new inventory of self-care tasks, most strikingly in areas of hygiene. Shaving has strong significance for male identification, and a girl proceeds, often self-consciously, to learn the art of applying cosmetics. This can involve delicate, precise motor tasks as in applying eye makeup and may require long hours of practice. Or, depending on current fads, the emphasis may be on a natural look. Likewise, hair styling commands major attention, and the adolescent, asserting his independence, resists adult intrusions on his individuality. In reality, his "individuality" may more accurately represent his attempt to pattern himself after a selected idol.

Clothing styles change rapidly, and for peer approval one's wardrobe must keep pace. Deviation singles one out as being "different." True individuality is more likely to be the exception as the adolescent strives to win approval from his peer group.

The list of tasks to be accomplished by the adolescent can be overwhelming when surveyed in a serious way by him. Some adolescents appear to give little thought to approaching responsibilities of adulthood; possibly such avoidance relieves anxiety which those responsibilities provoke. Adults can be helpful in giving reassurance and in organizing tasks. Assigned responsibility and level of expectation may need to be altered according to individual capacity. Learning to drive a car, perfect cooking skills and other homemaking arts, manage finances, experience work in an occupational capacity under supervision, and, above all, acquire ease in more intimate boy-girl relationships stress the strength of the adolescent's ego.

INTERRUPTIONS IN ACQUIRING INDEPENDENCE

It is evident that maturation of self-concepts, habits of industry, and relationships with others affect the child's motivational drive in attaining independence. Consider instead interruptions of the process. How does a physical handicap complicate the child's detachment from the mother? How does he acquire habits of industry if he lacks motors for movement? How does he learn to relate to others and acquire social skills if he is isolated from peer groups because of illness or disability? To what degree do pain and fatigue drain creative, emotional, and physical energy? What happens to his self-image when he suddenly becomes paralyzed from traumatic injury? For him there is the necessity of reconstituting a sense of self-worth and a new image he can accept.

COPING PATTERNS SEEN IN THE DISABLED CHILD

Coping has been described by Murphy (1962) as the process of developing ways of dealing with new and difficult situations. It is the manner by which the child comes to terms with challenges or makes use of an opportunity. *Adaptation* is the result.

The kinds of coping behavior exhibited by physically and developmentally handicapped children are not peculiar to them; they are similar to those shown by their nondisabled peers. However, the more severe the handicap is the greater the degree of dependency will be that is forced on the child and the more tenuous will be his means of meeting society's expectations for concealment of dependency needs.

In the process of growth the handicapped child's attitude toward himself contains a mixture of feelings. He may have a sense of inadequacy in coping with the environment. Barker and Wright (1953) describe the environmental reality, for the handicapped child, as a kind of physical anxiety, an uncertainty as to whether he will be able to carry out the locomotions, manipulations, and perceptions required in any one environment and which he must negotiate before he can achieve his set purposes, for example, shopping in a supermarket from a wheelchair. He may experience social anxiety because of the unstable perceptions others in his environment form about his disability as he comes in contact with them. Thus his own perceptions about himself are inconsistent. A distorted body image may lead to denial of disability or an exaggeration of the limitations imposed.

Behavioral responses in coping with disability evidently may be ineffective and maladaptive. A child may choose to cling to a more comfortable, regressed, immature level, finding greater gratification in his dependency; or he may dwell on his limitations and become withdrawn and depressed through his own self-absorption. Agression and hostility in some cases are directed inwardly or explode in misdirected ways.

The child's struggle with his body image and concept of self affects his attitude toward his family and their attitude toward him. According to Rusk and Taylor (1953), the handicapped child at an early age is given an unusual amount of help and attention from family members and thus receives social status and self-esteem. But as he becomes older, he imposes a greater burden on the family in terms of their time, physical management, accommodation of life-style, and money. This causes both resentment and guilt, and the child, being necessarily dependent, may suppress his blame; instead, he may exhibit self-hostility and guilt. At the other end of the spectrum, parents tend to overprotect the child, either from genuine sympathy and concern or as a result of guilt reaction.

A common anxiety of a child involved in treatment programs is a loss of participation in decision making. In a struggle to gain control, he may exhibit uncooperative, hostile behavior or verbalize that he does not care what happens to him. Other patients, overwhelmed by a sense of futility, become passive and lack a display of involvement.

In assessing the impact of disability on the child and his family, the health professional is challenged to separate out those behaviors which are appropriate and useful and those which are detrimental to the child's situation and disability status. Results of assessment should include, when necessary, recommendations for a program of modification or, at least, suggested ways to improve the patient's and family's handling of very difficult life adjustment. Most importantly, the assessor should attempt to identify the child's perceptions. Menninger (1953) counsels that "disability is not so much what the examiner perceives it to be, as it is what the patient perceives it to be."

CONCLUSION

Growth in independence is an unsteady process that draws from all developmental systems. Coping skills are essential in achieving independence and are acquired through experience—by imitation, through instruction, or by psychological osmosis—or simply become implanted through obscure means that defy analysis.

Assessing the effectiveness of coping skills and resulting adaptation is an unstructured part of the activities of daily living evaluation.

REFERENCES

Barker, R. G., and Wright, B. A. 1953. The social psychology of adjustment to physical disability. In Garrett, J. F., editor: Psychological aspects of physical disability. Rehabilitation Service Series No. 210. Washington, D.C., U.S. Department of Health, Education and Welfare.

Brazelton, T. B. 1969. Infants and mothers—differences in development. New York, Dell Publishing Co., Inc.,

Cohen, L. B., and Salapatek, P., editors. 1975. From sensation to cognition, Vols. I and II. New York, Academic Press, Inc.

Erikson, E. H. 1963. Childhood and society, ed. 2. New York, W. W. Norton & Co., Inc., Publishers.

Fraiberg, S. H. 1959. The magic years—understanding and handling the problems of early childhood. New York, Charles Scribner's Sons.

Gesell, A. 1940. The first five years of life—a guide to the study of the pre-school child. New York, Harper & Row, Publishers.

Gesell, A., and Ilg, F. L. 1943. Infant and child in the culture of today—the guidance of development in home and nursery school. New York, Harper & Row, Publishers.

Gillette, N. P. 1971. Occupational therapy and mental health. In Willard, H. S., and Spackman, C. S., editors: Occupational therapy. Philadelphia, J. B. Lippincott Co.

Josselyn, I. 1960. Treatment of the adolescent—some psychological aspects. Am. J. Occup. Ther. 14: 191-195.

Kent, C. A. 1971. Psychosocial development—function and dysfunction. In Banus, B. S.: The developmental therapist. Thorofare, N. J., Charles B. Slack, Inc.

Luria, A. R. 1960. The role of speech in the regulation of normal and abnormal behavior. Bethesda, Md., U.S. Department of Health, Education, and Welfare, Russian Scientific Translation Program.

Menninger, K. A. 1953. Psychiatric aspects of physical disability. In Garrett, J. F., editor: Psychological aspects of physical disability. Rehabilitation Service Series No. 210. Washington, D.C., U.S. Department of Health, Education and Welfare.

Murphy, L. B. 1962. The widening world of childhood—paths toward mastery. New York, Basic Books, Inc., Publishers.

Rusk, H. A., and Taylor, E. J. 1953. Team approach in rehabilitation and the psychologist's role. In Garrett, J. F., editor: Psychological aspects of physical disability. Rehabilitation Service Series No. 210. Washington, D.C., U.S. Department of Health, Education and Welfare.

Senn, M. J., and Solnit, A. J. 1968. Problems in child behavior and development. Philadelphia, Lea & Febiger.

Spitz, R. 1965. The first year of life—a psychoanalytic study of normal and deviant development of object relations. New York, International Universities Press, Inc.

Vander Veer, A. H. 1949. Occupational therapy in a children's hospital—a psychiatric viewpoint. Presented before the Tri-State Hospital Assembly, Palmer House, Chicago.

7 *Perception and self-care tasks*

PART I

An overview of perception—from sensation to sensory impression or motor response

In previous chapters brief reference has been made to perceptual requirements for performing self-care tasks. Now we shall examine the relationship between perception and function in more detail, utilizing basic neuroanatomical and neurophysiological information. Perception is an exceedingly involved subject, worthy of extended study, but this discussion has the specific objective of renewing the reader's awareness of perceptual behavior and clarifying how perception is essential for performing activities of daily living.

During the evaluation an assessor's ability to collect observations relating to perceptual skills is limited, in a sense, because the child's perceptual abilities may only become evident when there is dysfunction. Otherwise, the complex mechanisms are not distinctly obvious. The task for the assessor becomes one of identifying signals, then, when quantity and degree warrant, relaying them to a specialist qualified through certification and training to test the child with batteries and selected tools that measure the effectiveness and reliability of his sensory modalities.

An elementary review of perception makes more complex concepts plausible. When assessors understand where structures are, what they look like, and how they work, they are in a better position to understand relationships between them and theories about what these relationships mean. A good way to begin is to raise a few questions.

WHAT IS PERCEPTION?

Humans move, touch (and feel), see, hear, taste, and smell. All of these senses yield information about the environment. This information is transmitted to the brain or some other location in the central nervous system, and there, with the influence of past experience, it is integrated, allowing individuals to interpret their environment and interact with it, largely through muscular movement. Thus individuals "perceive," obtaining impressions through their senses. But the process is extremely complicated.

AN ILLUSTRATION

Before a child can master dressing tasks, it is understood that he must have the eye-hand coordination for manipulating fastenings. In addition, it is necessary for him to have a knowledge of his physical self and how body parts are related, that is, to have formulated a body scheme. He must know where his body is in space. As he attends to dressing tasks, he looks at body movements, kinesthetically he feels the position of body parts, and he may even verbalize motor actions aloud. He consciously directs some body movements, whereas others are automatic and compensatory, enabling him to maintain equilibrium in the various positions he assumes. He has an awareness of the two sides of his body and, because of neurological integration, is able to use his limbs cooperatively and reciprocally.

The child also looks at the clothing he will wear and, in doing so, distinguishes boundaries of an article. He visually scans for details, and as the attention and focus of his eyes shift selectively, he separates foreground and background. Discriminatively, he recognizes the form and totality of an article of clothing and categorizes it, either as a sweater, shirt, sock, or other item. This is an extension of the sensory process, involving concept formation. Having identified the article, he maintains a visual form constancy of it, even if it is turned upside down. Through experience he accumulates space ideas.

The motor components of dressing can be observed and, consequently, are more readily comprehended. What is less clearly understood are the internal mechanisms at work—the way the child receives and processes sensory information leading to his response in attending to the task at hand. All self-care activities require sensory organization within the central nervous system.

To explore and attempt to understand perception, let us begin with the body.

CONCEPTS OF THE BODY

Concepts of one's body evolve slowly from birth and are influenced by all other developmental processes. Terms for body concepts include *body scheme, body concept, body image,* and, in a related sense, *self-image* and *self-concept.*

In her investigations of perceptions, Ayres (1964) made reference to the work of the neurologist, Henry Head, who in 1920 conceived of the body scheme as a postural model against which the organism can measure changes in position and movement. The preceding discussion of dressing tasks outlines the child's need for a knowledge of his physical self, relationships of parts, and the way in which the child's body potentially can deal with space. The child visualizes his body and movements in parts of it.

Body image is sometimes used interchangeably with body scheme, but it appears to be a more inclusive concept, composed of interpersonal, environmental, and temporal factors. It has been used previously in the handbook with this connotation, along with the terms self-concept and body concept. Frostig and Maslow (1970) describe body concept more exactingly as the factual knowledge of the body, that is, a human being has two eyes, one nose, two arms, and so on.

Knickerbocker (1966) unifies body scheme and body image through an evolutionary description: "In the creation of body schema, all senses are collaborating. Body image is an outgrowth of this sensory input."*

At the same time, the child develops space concepts and motor control of position orientation (up, down, front, back, etc.). This learning, plus control, serves as a basis for planning movement. Because the child observes his body movements and feels them, he first develops space concepts in relation to his own body and its movements. Gradually he is able to identify these orientations in the body of another person. Visually, he notes spatial relationships and appraises distance and direction from himself and, later, of one object in relation to another. Slowly he constructs a "space world" around him. Ayres, Knickerbocker, and others describe the process, but how does it come about?

Much that is known revolves around theoretical data, gathered through careful investigation. Consensus is variable, partially because neurological knowledge changes as new studies are completed. From a purely scientific standpoint there is still no known basis for learning, and according to Ayres (1958), considerable data demonstrate that much of the perceptual process is learned.

It can be said that the earliest influences in the development of body scheme are probably tactile and kinesthetic. Rosen (1966) explains that as the infant begins to move, he acquires knowledge of his body through sensory stimuli, particularly from his hands (tactile) and also from impressions from the vestibular apparatus and the receptors in muscles and joints. Awareness of internal organs is gained from sensations of discomfort. According to Rosen the progressively developed images of the body and its parts are implanted as memory traces within the nervous system. Thus perception begins with sensations.

HOW SENSATIONS ARE GATHERED

An individual receives stimuli from his internal and external environment through structures called sensory receptors. These sensory receptors have been described by Wyke (1975) as continually "scanning" the world in which the body lives and moves and has its being. A sensory receptor may be a cell or group of cells, a sense organ, or a sense nerve ending. Depending on its threshold, a stimulated receptor gives rise to a sensory message in the form of an impulse. Receptors may be located throughout the body or, according to type, are limited to a relatively small body area. There are several methods of grouping receptors; for example, they may be classified according to the type of energy required to produce the stimulus (mechanoreceptors, thermoreceptors, chemoreceptors) or by location in the body (exteroceptors, interoceptors, proprioceptors).

---

*From Knickerbocker, B. M. 1966. The significance of body scheme and body image in perceptual-motor dysfunction. Proceedings of Ohio Occupational Therapy Association Conference on Body Image, Cleveland.

Exteroceptors

Exteroceptors are located on or near the surface of the body and receive stimuli of the outside world. Stimuli, or environmental energy, may be present in the form of mechanical vibrations as with sound waves or pressure waves, as chemical changes in the environment, or through electromagnetic waves including light rays. For example, the eye has optic receptors, the sensitive rods and cones of the retina that receive light rays. The ear has auditory receptors within the inner ear that respond to air vibrations. The vibrations enter through the external auditory canal and are subsequently transmitted through perilymph fluid to tiny hairlike receptors, the organs of Corti, located within the cochlea.

Receptors in the tongue, or taste buds, detect chemical stimuli. There are at least four types of taste buds, and although all can respond to more than one of the basic taste stimuli, each type responds most strongly to one of them. It has been generally accepted that sweet and salty tastes are most effectively identified at the tip of the tongue, sour taste at the sides of the tongue, and bitter taste at the back part of the tongue. Now some authorities believe that taste buds may be scattered around the oral cavity—in the soft and hard palates, the upper throat, and along the gums. Regardless of their location, taste buds are stimulated only if substances to be tasted are in solution.

Smell is also a chemical sense and, to arouse the sensation, a substance must first be in a gaseous state, then be dissolved in the mucus secreted by the nasal mucous membrane. Receptors for smell are located in the upper part of the nasal cavity in the olfactory epithelium. Because the receptors are high in the upper cleft, one may "sniff" an odor to bring the gases responsible for it upward in the nose.

The exteroceptors described thus far respond only to special stimuli—light rays, sound waves, chemicals—and are limited in distribution to a relatively small area of the body. Other exteroceptors respond to general sensations such as warmth, cold, pain, or touch and are scattered throughout the body. They may also be referred to as contact receptors. At one time it was thought that each type of cutaneous sensation had its particular receptor which responded selectively to environmental changes. Now it is believed that although some specialization may exist, these receptors respond to various sensations. Some authorities emphasize that morphologically humans have no specific terminals for cutaneous sensations and, additionally, each point on the skin has multiple innervations.

Among the receptors found in the dermis are Meissner's corpuscles, small oval structures found in the hands, feet, lips, mucous membranes of the tongue, areas sensitive to light touch, and certain other parts of the body. Other oval bodies found in the subcutaneous tissue of the fingers are called brushes of Ruffini, after the individual who first described them. Still another receptor body having a wider distribution in surface area is the Krause end bulb, a capsule variable in shape from oval to cylindrical. Continued stimulation of general sensory receptors, as with other sensory organs, causes them to adapt to the stimuli so that with sustained input the individual does not feel a sensation as acutely as when originally presented.

The receptors for pain are the most widely distributed sensory end organs and are the most protective sense. They are found in the skin, muscles, and joints and to a lesser extent in most internal organs, including blood vessels and viscera. Pain receptors are not oval bodies as many of the other sensory end organs but apparently merely branchings of the nerve fibers, called free nerve endings. Unlike other senses, pain sense does not readily adapt to continued stimulation. The threshold of irritability for reception is high; consequently, the stimulations are of such intensity as to be a threat. As a result, responsive receptors are frequently called nociceptors (*nocere*, to injure). They elicit protective and defensive reflexes, and because of their vital importance, the impulses from nociceptors are always given right-of-way in their passage through the nervous system (Zoethout and Tuttle, 1958).

Most pain sensations are derived from receptors in the skin. There are two kinds of pain detected through exteroceptors: deep pain, which is diffuse, throbbing, and longer lasting; and sharp pain, which is well localized and sharp.

Interoceptors

Interoceptors are located in viscera—body organs such as the stomach and intestines; they are thought to be present in blood vessels as well. Interoceptors respond to internal stimuli: pain that is diffuse and nonspecific, and stretch and contraction to an abnormal degree.

Proprioceptors

Proprioceptors (*proprio*, oneself) react to stimuli arising within body tissue: skeletal muscles, joints, tendons, fascia, and ligaments. They are the sense organs stimulated by movement of the body itself. They make individuals aware of the movement or position of the body in space and of the various parts of the body to each other. Sensations that arise include deep pressure, changes in muscular tensions, and equilibrium. Muscle sense organs play an important part in maintaining muscle tone and posture patterns, as well as allowing for the adjustments of the muscles for the particular kind of work to be done.

Muscle and tendon receptors

Embedded among skeletal muscle fibers are structures called neuromuscular spindles, which contain sensory receptors. A neuromuscular spindle is made up of intrafusal fibers, as opposed to extrafusal fibers of surrounding muscle tissue. The sensory receptors in the neuromuscular spindle are of two types, each with its particular threshold to stretch; spindles are both a sensory and motor mechanism. The interplay is complex and involves the stretch reflex and alpha and gamma motor neurons. Opinions differ regarding the mechanism, but whatever process occurs, the result of the interplay is a continuous altering of muscle tone to fit varying circumstances.

Another receptor, the neurotendinous spindle (organs of Golgi), is found at the junction of tendon and muscle or sometimes within a muscle sheath. It serves to provide information relative to the static tension and tension changes in the muscle itself. This tendon organ has a high threshold for a stretch stimulus and characteristically responds only when a muscle is stretched beyond the maximum length it normally assumes. If this limit is exceeded, the organ then acts in an inhibitory capacity to the muscle in which it lies and prevents muscle tearing. On the other hand, the threshold for contraction is apparently low. Therefore the neurotendinous spindle reacts more readily to the tension created by muscle contraction and, through its inhibitory influence, regulates the strength of the contraction.

More about muscle tone

The proprioceptors assist in maintaining muscle tone and increasing the ability to maintain a contraction. Muscle tone refers to a partially contracted state of muscles. All living muscles normally possess tonus to some degree because of gravity or the action of opposing (antagonist) muscles; for example, tonus can be felt in muscles that support the weight of an outstretched arm against the pull of gravity. Even a normal, live muscle that appears to be fully relaxed still possesses a small amount of tension. Some authorities believe that this is related to the reflex activity of the nervous system (Gatz, 1973); others point to the quality of firmness as a manifestation of normal elasticity and turgor of muscle tissue.

Tonic contractions are sometimes spoken of as static or postural contraction in distinction to phasic contractions, which bring about movements of parts of the body; phasic contractions may be reflex or volitional.

Muscle tone serves the important purpose of maintaining body posture. The antigravity muscles have more tonus than the other muscles. Impulses responsible for muscle tonus, the tension necessary for maintaining posture and equilibrium, are derived not only from proprioceptors in muscles and tendons but also from the mechanisms for equilibrium and from visual stimulation.

Special proprioceptors

The "special" proprioceptors of the body are found in the nonauditory part of the inner ear, the labyrinth. They are stimulated by movements or change of position of the head in space. Three semicircular canals lying at right angles to each other extend out from and return to the central structure, or vestibule. At the base of the fluid-filled canals is a bulblike enlargement, the ampulla, which is where the sensory equipment for the canals is located. The basal structure is the crista acoustica, a gelatinous mass with ciliated structures. This mass moves freely, depending on the movements of the fluid, the endolymph. The movement, in turn, stimulates hair processes and hair cells in the crista. These hair cells are the rotary receptors and are stimulated both by angular acceleration or rotation. Because of the physical orientation of the three canals, the movement within any of the three ampullae will depend on the plane in which movement occurs. Each is maximally stimulated when the plane of rotation corresponds to its plane of orientation (Mueller, 1965).

A similar kind of sensory epithelium is found in the utricle and saccule lying in the central structure. The fluid here contains a number of particles, formed of a calcium compound. These small concretions are known as otoliths, or ear stones, which are heavier than the fluid in which they are immersed and therefore rest on the hairlike endings in the epithelial walls, the macula acoustica. Their position on the macula is determined by the orientation of the head in space and linear acceleration.

Conscious stimuli

Much of the proprioceptor and interoceptor information never rises to consciousness. However, consciousness for pressure exists even when skin is anesthetized. The pressure end organs, the Pacinian corpuscles, are located in subcutaneous and deeper tissues and around joints and are sometimes referred to as receptors for deep touch. They are stimulated by pressure of surrounding structures when joints are moved. This contributes to an individual's kinesthetic sense, that is, one's position sense and changes in the location of parts with respect to each other. Individuals "feel" the degree to which the fingers are bent or an arm is extended. Mueller (1965) explains kinesthetic sense in a more exacting manner. A person knows where his body is in space because individual sensory nerve cells seem to be sharply tuned to a certain range of angles. Correspondingly, they send out sensory impulses when a joint is at a particular range or passes through a particular position. Collectively, the nerve fibers coming from the joints are capable of registering any given position of the limb.

The stimulus for "touch" sensation is the deforming of the skin by unequal pressure. Tactile sensitivity is at the highest degree in the fingertips and lips. There is also a sense of locality for touch; that is, a person can tell more or less accurately when the skin is touched. Normally, when two widely separated areas of the skin are stimulated simultaneously, two sensations are experienced and can be discriminated. As was learned earlier, the skin responds to various classes of stimuli; things may feel rough or smooth, warm or cold, vibratory or steady. Reception of information from sense organs in the skin contributes to three-dimensional information and discrimination of weight, shape, and texture, but other stimuli contribute as well, such as vision and muscle-joint sense. Complex processes are involved, including the correlating of past information with the present stimulus, which occurs in many parts of the nervous system at once.

HOW SENSATIONS ARE PROCESSED AND ACTED ON

The stimulation of a sensory receptor informs the nervous system of environmental changes to which adaptive adjustments must be made, in some instances for the preservation of life (Zoethout and Tuttle, 1958). Numerous impulses, occurring simultaneously, arrive within the central nervous system and are filtered, collated, and integrated according to the needs of the organism. A review of some principal participating structures is presented now, beginning with the functional unit of the nervous system, the neuron.

The neuron

Stimulation of a receptor will initiate an electrical change or impulse, which travels from the receptor site to a specific part of the body by way of a chain of neurons. A neuron is a nerve cell body with all of its processes. To visualize this structure, consider that an average neuron (nerve cell body) is slightly less than 0.1 mm in diameter, just below the visual range of the naked eye (Dethier and Stellar, 1970), but the delicate processes (also invisible) range in length from fractions of an inch to several feet. The nerve fibers are of two types: dendrites, which conduct impulses to the cell body; and longer axons, which conduct impulses away from the body. The rate at which impulses travel along the nerve fibers depends on the diameter of the fiber; the larger the fiber the greater will be the rate of conduction, other factors remaining the same.

Nerve cell bodies are usually located in groups; outside the brain and spinal cord these groups are called ganglia. Similar clusters of nerve cell bodies inside the brain and spinal cord are known as nuclei. In the cortex of the cerebrum and cerebellum, they are arranged in layers where they serve as integrative and transmission centers of great complexity.

At the point where the termination of an axon of one neuron comes in close proximity with the cell body or dendrites of another, the impulse traveling in the first neuron initiates an impulse in the second neuron across a "synaptic" junction. The impulse is perpetuated from one synapse to another by electrochemical changes, constituting a membrane change, a chemical change, and an electrical change. It is believed that when an impulse reaches a synapse, it causes the release at the nerve ending of a chemical substance which bridges the gap and forms the stimulus to conduct the impulse to the next neuron. Synapses are polarized, and impulses pass in one direction only. They are susceptible to fatigue and extremely susceptible to the effects of oxygen deficiency, anesthetics, and other agents. The function of a synapse is to serve as a point of communication. Although they have a common function, synapses are not alike. Dethier and Stellar (1970) explain that they vary in size, location on the nerve cell, and in chemical composition. These differences contribute to many possible kinds of connections. Many axons may impinge on a single cell, or an axon may branch profusely and synapse with many cells. A tight arrangement, such as exists in nuclei, enhances the number of possible connections in a given space.

Synapses provide a structure of variable resistance to transmission of impulses. Consistently an impulse follows the pathway of least neural resistance, yet inhibition at the synapse predominates over excitation. Resistance at the synapse may be altered by the number of impulses coming to it. Although impulses do not waver in intensity, they reinforce one another to propagate an impulse. This manner of reinforcement is called *summation* and results in facilitation.

As noted, an impulse travels along a neuron chain between the receptor and effector. Neurons lying in between are called interneurons, or internuncials, and make up fiber tracts.

There is an additional kind of cell in the brain called the glia cell. This is a non-nervous cell serving as supportive tissue, or "filler." Glia cells are considerably more numerous than nerve cells, and some authorities suggest that they may possibly fill a role in memory storage.

The nerve

When nerve fibers make up a bundle of fibers outside the central nervous system, they constitute a nerve. Nerves carrying impulses to the spinal cord and brain are called *afferent* nerves, and ones relaying impulses back to muscles and glands are *efferent* nerves. A nerve may carry both afferent and efferent impulses, serving as a *mixed* nerve. Nerves are connectors between the brain and spinal cord and various parts of the body. They are not equally excitable to stimuli at all times. Even though a stimulus may be constant, nerve impulses occur as pulses not as a continuous signal.

Peripheral nervous system

Impulses travel to and from the central nervous system (the brain and spinal cord) through cranial and spinal nerves that comprise the peripheral nervous system. Fibers of peripheral nerves are the processes of neurons whose cell bodies are located either within the brain, spinal cord, or in ganglia.

Cranial nerves (twelve pairs in number) have their origin in the brain. Many of the names listed* imply their destination or function, but function becomes most evident when a disturbance occurs.

First cranial nerve (olfactory)—Loss or disturbance of sense of smell. Especially significant is a unilateral loss of smell without intranasal explanation.

Second cranial nerve (optic)—Blindness of various types. Loss of visual acuity unassociated with a refractive error.

Third, fourth, and sixth cranial nerves (oculomotor, trochlear, and abducent)— Drooping of upper lid (ptosis). Deficiencies in movement or abnormalities in parallelism of eyes.

Fifth cranial nerve (trigeminal)—Weakness, atrophy of temporalis, masseter and pterygoid muscles. Difficulty chewing. Loss of sensation, or presence of pain, in face, forehead, temple, and eye.

Seventh cranial nerve (facial)—Loss of facial expression. Inability to wrinkle forehead, to close eyes, or to whistle. Unilateral paralysis causing deviation of mouth toward the sound side.

Eighth cranial nerve (auditory)—Deafness or a disturbance of hearing such as ringing in either ear. Dizziness, nausea, and vomiting. (This nerve has two divisions, the auditory and the vestibular, and may be referred to as "vestibulocochlear.")

Ninth and tenth cranial nerves (glossopharyngeal and vagus)—Disturbance of taste (posterior tongue). Reduced gag. Difficulty in swallowing. (The two nerves overlap in this function.) Disturbance to the vagus nerve may also result in hoarseness, difficulty in talking (vocal cords), and reduced strength of cough.

Eleventh cranial nerve (spinal accessory)—Inability to turn face to one side. Drooping of shoulder.

*Modified from Van Allen, M. W. 1969. Pictorial manual of neurologic tests. Chicago, Year Book Medical Publishers, Inc.

Twelfth cranial nerve (hypoglossal)—Paralysis of one side of tongue with deviation toward paralyzed side. Tremors (fasciculations) of tongue at rest. Thick speech.

Spinal nerves (thirty-one) carry impulses to and from the spinal cord. They are mixed nerves, conducting both afferent and efferent impulses. Just after passing through the intervertebral foramina, a spinal nerve separates into posterior and anterior roots. All fibers conveying sensory impulses enter the cord through the posterior roots of the spinal nerves, whereas the anterior roots are channels for nerve fibers carrying outgoing motor impulses from the anterior horns of the spinal cord. Each motor neuron in the anterior horn serves as the pathway for motor impulses initiated in higher motor centers in the cerebrum, and it also receives relays of afferent impulses from other reflex centers in the spinal cord. Thus it serves as a "final common pathway" for which impulses may compete. Allied ones may reinforce each other, but as we have learned, protective motor responses take precedence. To further illustrate the intricacy of the neural system, one can visualize that each axon of a lower motor neuron divides into many branches and each branch ends at a *motor end-plate* of a single muscle fiber. The motor nerve with the group of muscle fibers it supplies is called *the motor unit*.

Certain peripheral nerves have a special function and together comprise the *autonomic nervous system*, a functional division that innervates smooth and cardiac muscle and the glands of the body. It operates at the subconscious level and is integrated with other body activities. Specifically, actions of the heart muscle, smooth musculature of the blood vessels, gastrointestinal tract, uterus, and bladder depend on autonomic impulses.

The autonomic nervous system is further divided into the *sympathetic* and *parasympathetic* systems. When stimulated, the sympathetic system acts as an accelerator, mobilizing resources to prepare the body for emergencies as in conditions of stress. It regulates the composition, temperature, quantity, and distribution of the fluid medium of the body's cells. When it acts, the intake of oxygen through the respiratory system is increased, circulation is raised to maximal efficiency, blood glucose is mobilized to provide fuel for strenuous activity, the pupils of the eyes are dilated, and the body is ready for defensive action (Gotten and Wilson, 1949).

The parasympathetic system normally acts as a balance for the sympathetic system, restoring the body to a stabilized state. It reacts locally rather than generally. As a reparative influence, it contributes to the appropriate digestion, absorption, and elimination of food by providing for the flow of saliva and gastric juices and increasing the tonic state of the gastrointestinal tract. Through vagus impulses the heart rate is slowed, thereby providing rest and recuperation. Pupils of the eyes are narrowed, protecting the retina from excessive light. Such influences tend to counterbalance the activity of the sympathetic division when the danger is past.

Stimulation of the parasympathetic system and inhibition of the sympathetic system and vice versa have the same overall effects.

Central nervous system

Despite a vast accumulation of knowledge, much of the human brain remains inscrutable and inaccessible. Therefore the brain continues to be a subject for speculation and disagreement. A great quantity of the information that is available is from research on animals, gathered through ablation, electrical recording, and artifical stimulation. Accepted scientific facts provide a body of knowledge and, in turn, a framework for understanding some of the complex mechanisms of the brain, as well as giving substance for the formation of theories. For example, something is known of the magnitude of impulses flowing to the brain by way of the spinal cord and cranial nerves. It is believed that as many as 100,000 neurons may be involved in transmitting the information that results in an action as simple as stepping back to avoid being struck by an oncoming vehicle. Investigators know, more certainly, that the process occurs in less than a second. Given such an illustration, certain assumptions can be made; for example, reinforcement and inhibition of impulses are vital in protecting the organism, and organization of impulses is necessary to preserve stability. Other conclusions may appear almost simplistic; for instance, memory in the form of retained impressions of previous stimuli plays a role in influencing responses. Yet this information is the result of extensive studies, and an analysis reveals complex processes at work.

One aspect of brain function that arouses a great deal of interest is *integration*. Although evidence of integration can be cited, at this point in time the precise manner by which neural activity is integrated has not been determined, and there is no identifiable "integrative center." Rather, evidence points toward the newer structures of the neocortex as directing activity, whereas older structures at the brain stem level modulate and coordinate sensory impulses and motor responses subcortically. Even a reflex arc at the spinal cord level represents a form of integration.

More recently, older structures have received increased attention by the occupational therapy profession. Ayres (1972), Moore (1976), and others emphasize the significance of neural activity that occurs within the reticular formation and the limbic system. Ayres suggests that both systems are fundamentally integrating mechanisms.

Moore believes biasing or reinforcement of behavioral drives may be accomplished primarily at the limbic level. This system, comprising parts of the old and new cerebral cortex as well as brain stem structures, is thought to "move" and drive humans so that they can survive as individuals and as a species. This involves memory, emotion, visceral functions, and olfaction.

Some neurologists consider the reticular formation as the master control mechanism in the central nervous system. The ascending portion, called the *reticular activating system*, is a diffuse, sensory arousal system located at the core of the brain stem, just above the spinal cord and below the thalamus and hypothalamus. Sensory impulses synapse here, within a meshwork of intermingling and interconnecting neurons that run on up to the midline region of the thalamus and from there to all parts of the cerebral cortex and other parts of the brain. The information transmitted does not seem to preserve receptor-surface locus or sensory modality (Dethier and Stellar, 1970). The impulses are unspecified messages, signaling the presence of some kind of stimulation and alerting the cortex that news is on its way. Discriminatory powers are thereby enhanced, and consequently the cortex is better able to deal with and process "specific" information arriving over the specific sensory input channels to the cortex (Hilgard and Bower, 1975). Although the reticular activating system regulates incoming sensory input, it is always under the influence of the cortical processes so that there is a constant reciprocal influence between the conscious and subconscious structures.

Ayres (1972) proposes that investigators look toward normalizing reticular formation activity, since higher levels do not function optimally without adequate lower function, and all complex perceptual tasks depend on the cortex. This idea, along with many others she has presented to fellow professionals, is challenging to consider. If one is really to understand proposed principles, it becomes necessary to study the nervous system, tediously and methodically, and respond to simple, basic questions: What are the gross structures of the central nervous system? Where do specific impulses travel? What is the result of particular kinds of stimuli? The discussion that follows will address itself to such questions within a limited depth.

A journey

An impulse begins its journey from the receptor site and, unless involved in a simple reflex arc, travels to various levels in the central nervous system, depending on the origin of the impulse and the type of message carried. It travels upward through rather specific ascending neural pathways, or tracts, within the spinal cord. A tract consists of nerve fibers that have a common origin and a common destination. When the impulse arrives within the central nervous system, it is processed at incomprehensible speed and filtered through a synaptic system of checks and balances. Although the impulse may be especially mediated at a particular center in the central nervous system, it is understood that the brain responds as a whole, as a unified network. This requires neural communication from one neuron to another and from one side of the brain to the other, to higher and lower levels. The impulse, a message, is filtered through synapses between neurons and dispensed to various locations. Theoretically, an impulse traveling over any given sensory fiber can be transmitted to any and all efferent neurons, which are about five times fewer in number than afferent neurons, but graded synaptic resistance provides the guide and protects the organism. Huss (1971) explains how this occurs: "Each neuron has a threshold, which is the amount of electrical energy required to cause a propagation of the impulse. If the resting threshold is too high or the stimulus raises the threshold, then the neuron is said to be inhibited. If the threshold lowers so that it is more easily fired off or fires automatically, then it is said to be facilitated."* Both inhibition and facilitation are

*From Huss, A. J. 1971. Sensorimotor treatment approaches. In Willard, H. S., and Spackman, C. S., editors: Occupational therapy, ed. 4, p. 387. Philadelphia, J. B. Lippincott Co.

necessary in controlling the vast amount of stimuli bombarding the central nervous system at any one time, and together they preserve homeostasis.

Some impulses travel to the highest level of the brain, the cortex, where they become conscious stimuli. Below the cortex they are unconscious stimuli to the organism or may be said to be subcortical or subliminal. Impulses regulated at these levels tend to produce more stereotyped and automatic responses such as are seen in the newborn. As noted earlier, a child's nervous system is not fully mature at birth, although most authorities agree that the complete number of neurons is present. Pathways, or connections between the neurons, are not fully established, particularly within the cortex. The rate and exact pattern of neurobiological maturation represents another area of divergent opinion.

Moore (1973) counsels that in the mature nervous system "one cannot state that a reflex 'belongs to' or is confined at a certain central nervous system level. The entire nervous system is involved in all reflexes to a greater or lesser degree, especially when man is concerned."* However, reflexes are commonly associated with particular levels. For example, the cerebrum and cerebellum most closely regulate equilibrium reactions; the brain stem, including the midbrain, mediates the righting reactions, tonic neck reflexes, positive and negative supporting reflexes, and associated reactions. Vital reflexes related to swallowing, gag, vomiting, and other physiological activities are controlled at centers in the medulla of the brain stem. Still other reflex centers are at the spinal cord level such as the myotatic or tendon stretch reflex and the flexor withdrawal, extensor thrust, and crossed extension reflexes. However, even at this level of more primitive neural function, higher centers potentially play a part in regulation.

Myelination, the formation of a fatty insulating sheath around nerves, is not complete in the newborn. The process is rapid during the first 2 years of life but slows thereafter. Even after being completely covered, growth in thickness of the sheath continues for years. A myelin sheath has nodes (nodes of Ranvier), and an impulse is propagated from node to node, thereby increasing the speed of impulse conduction. The largest myelinated fibers conduct at a rate of about 120 meters per second (270 miles per hour) and the smallest ones at about 6 meters per second (13½ miles per hour).

Ayres (1972) joins others in advising that investigators should consider a response as coming from the total central nervous system, since most, if not all, of the entire brain is involved to a varying degree because of the number of neural mechanisms at work there. What are these structures and mechanisms within the central nervous system that interact in producing a motor response to a sensory impulse?

The nervous system in human beings develops in the embryo from a simple tube of ectoderm, the primitive neural tube. The cells lining it become the nervous tissue of the brain and spinal cord, whereas the canal becomes distended to form the ven-

*From Moore, J. C. 1973. Sensorimotor integration, a workshop. San Diego, University of California Extension.

Forebrain		Midbrain	Hindbrain	
Telencephalon	Diencephalon	Mesencephalon	Metencephalon	Myelencephalon
cerebrum	thalamus hypothalamus	corpora quadrigemina	pons varolii cerebellum	medulla oblongata

Other divisions:

Basal ganglia: four masses of gray matter deep in the cerebral hemispheres:
   caudate, lentiform, amygdaloid nuclei, claustrum

Brain stem: considered by some authorities as those structures below the
   cerebrum except the cerebellum

Fig. 7-1. Phylogeny of the human brain. (Modified from Schottelius, B. A., and Schottelius, D. D.: Textbook of physiology, ed. 17, St. Louis, 1973, The C. V. Mosby Co.)

tricles of the brain and the central canal of the spinal cord. As layer on layer of cells develop, structures become more elaborate and complex. Fig. 7-1 illustrates the phylogeny. The divisions should be viewed as anatomical entities only, since the action of the nervous system biochemically and physiologically is integrated into an organized whole, serving the behavioral adaptations of the organism (Dethier and Stellar, 1970).

Structures and mechanisms of the brain

Cerebrum. The cerebrum is the largest part of the brain. It consists of two hemispheres whose surfaces are thrown into numerous folds or convolutions. This convoluted surface, called the cortical gray matter or cortex (bark), contains millions of neurons arranged in layers. About 90% of all nerve cells are in the cerebral cortex.

Beneath this neural mantle white matter lies in the interior of the hemispheres. The white matter consists of processes either of cortical cells or of cells located in the central gray matter (nuclei) of the brain stem. The fibers are of three types:

Projection fibers—carry impulses from the brain stem to the cortex and from the the cortex to the lower parts of the central nervous system.
Association fibers—originate in cortical cells and carry impulses to other areas of the cortex on the same side.
Transverse (commissural) fibers—carry impulses from one hemisphere to the other, forming a link between right and left sides of the cortex.

Research studies have established that all areas of the cortex do not perform the same function (Fig. 7-2). Topography reflecting this has been attempted by investigators, among them von Economo and Brodmann. We will now consider these functional areas of the cerebral cortex through the method of grouping them as "receiving" and "initiating" centers. An examination of the literature will reveal,

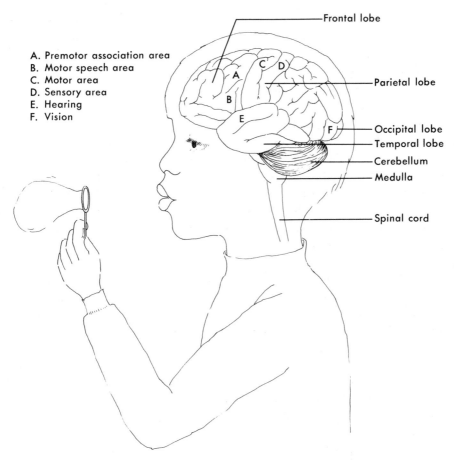

A. Premotor association area
B. Motor speech area
C. Motor area
D. Sensory area
E. Hearing
F. Vision

Frontal lobe
Parietal lobe
Occipital lobe
Temporal lobe
Cerebellum
Medulla
Spinal cord

Fig. 7-2. The brain as seen from the left side, illustrating the localization of cerebral functions. (Drawing by Florence Fujimoto.)

however, that researchers continue to challenge past information, and neurological maps are subject to change.

RECEIVING CENTERS FOR INCOMING INFORMATION TO THE CORTEX

Sensory receptive area. The sensory area, called the *somesthetic area,* is located in the parietal lobe. It receives proprioceptive impulses from the muscles, the impulses from the touch, heat, and cold receptors of the skin, and the deep sensibilities from the underlying tissues. This area receives impulses by which individuals become aware of the position of their limbs in space, of the particular area of the skin stimulated, of the number of discrete points of the skin stimulated, and of the relative weight of an object placed on the supported hand.

HOW IMPULSES ARE RELAYED TO THE SENSORY RECEPTIVE AREA. Impulses from proprioceptive end organs may or may not reach the sensory area. Receptor organs include the neuromuscular and neurotendinous spindles and the Pacinian corpuscles between muscles and in joint capsules. The impulses enter the spinal cord by way of dorsal root fibers. After entering the cord, the fibers continue in three divergent routes as described by Gatz (1973): Afferent fibers involved in a stretch reflex synapse with motor cells in the anterior horn cells within one or two spinal segments of the level at which they enter the cord; other fibers travel in several different pathways to the cerebellum; and a third group of fibers turn directly upward to reach the somesthetic area of the cerebral cortex by relay nuclei.

Special proprioceptive end organs in the labyrinth of the semicircular canals send impulses through fibers of the vestibular nerve, whose nuclei are clustered in the lateral part of the floor of the fourth ventricle. A few fibers pass directly to the cerebellum. Others synapse at the vestibular nuclei and descend with motor impulses to the spinal cord, where they assist local myotatic stretch reflexes. These impulses reinforce tonus of the extensor muscles of the limbs, producing enough extra force to support the body against gravity in an upright posture (Gatz, 1973). Synapses at the vestibular nuclei also contribute to muscular movements of the eyes and aid in balance.

Pain and temperature pathways reach the somesthetic area. Pain fibers enter the spinal cord in the lateral part of the dorsal root zone. After crossing they turn upward and continue without interruption through the spinal cord, pons, and midbrain to the thalamus, where they synapse and continue through the internal capsule to the sensory area (Gatz, 1973).

Touch sensations are more complex and involve two forms of touch sensibility. Simple touch is concerned with the sense of light touch and light pressure and a crude sense of tactile localization. Tactile discrimination conveys the sense of deeper pressure and spatial localization and the perception of size and shape of objects. After considerable longitudinal dispersion, synapsing and crossing, fibers take a direct upward course to reach the thalamus and sensory area of the cortex.

Visual receptive area. The visual area in the occipital lobe receives impulses from the retina. Axons of the neurons form the optic nerves, which, in turn, become the optic tracts. Impulses received in the posterior portion of the occipital lobe are primarily concerned with macular vision, where visual acuity is sharpest; the more anterior portion receives impulses from the peripheral fields. One side of the occipital area receives impressions from the field of vision on the opposite side, and images from both eyes are integrated into a single sensation. Adjoining areas in the occipital lobe are important regions for visual perception.

Auditory receptive area. The auditory area is located in the temporal lobe. It receives auditory radiations from the medial geniculate body, properly considered to be a part of the thalamus. This body serves as an auditory sensory relay center, conveying impulses from the cochlea of each ear. Stimulations of the region near the auditory receptive area cause buzzing and roaring sensations. Intelligent recognition of a particular sound depends on the auditory associative cortex.

Olfactory receptive area. The olfactory area is also located in the temporal lobe. Impulses travel in the first cranial nerve to the cerebrum. The olfactory system is the only sensory system that sends direct impulses to the cortex without utilizing the thalamus as a relay center.

Feedback loops. Sensory systems are continually active throughout the central nervous system. They not only provide information that results in a motor response but additionally provide feedback to the nervous system on the responses carried out. Subsequently, future motor output can be modulated because of the sensory effects of previous motor activity. The relationship between sensory and motor systems is therefore always influential in either direction. This kind of reciprocation is sometimes referred to as feedback loops or servomechanisms. With this in mind let us consider the elements making up the motor responses.

INITIATING CENTERS FOR OUTGOING MESSAGES FROM THE CORTEX

Motor area. The motor area is located in the frontal lobe and is thought by some authorities to correspond generally to the distribution of the giant pyramidal (Betz) cells. Motor impulses originating in this Brodmann's area initiate voluntary movement of skeletal muscle. One cerebral hemisphere controls the muscles on the opposite side of the body. Neurons in the motor cortex are devoted to body parts in a significant proportion. Large numbers of neurons are devoted to muscles of the hands and of articulation, which permits complicated movement and the acquisition of highly intricate skills.

Descending fibers of the motor area make up the pyramidal system, which goes from the motor cortex to motor nerves of the spinal cord and is highly specific. The path over which impulses must travel from the motor cortex to striated muscle is generally considered to have two components: upper motor neurons, which conduct impulses from the motor cortex to anterior horn cells of the gray matter, and lower motor neurons, which start in the anterior horn of the cord and end in the motor end-plate.

The smooth regulation of muscle action initiated in the motor cortex involves cooperation from several sources: the vestibular system together with proprioception, the cerebellar system, and a contribution from both these sources and other areas through the "extrapyramidal" system. This is thought to be a mechanism for motor facilitation at the premotor and motor cortex as well as at lower neuron sites in the spinal cord. The way in which the system operates is unclear. Dethier and Stellar (1970) describe it as a pathway made up of short neurons that make connections at many levels of the brain before reaching the motor nerve cells of the spinal cord. Its effect is a steadying one, serving to maintain an organized background of posture and muscle tone against which discrete localized movements mediated by the pyramidal paths can occur. When the system is damaged, varying types of rigidity, tremor, and uncoordinated muscle movement occur.

Premotor area. A premotor area lying anterior to the motor area in the frontal lobe is believed to act as a control of the motor area through an association process. It is involved in planning movement by correlating past experience with present stimuli. Part of one premotor area (the left one in right-handed persons) becomes the motor center for speech.

Speech area. Speech is a complicated development of the cerebral centers, being essentially a process that is learned. The localization of speech function cannot be limited to any group of cells, although as discussed previously, there are centers in the cortex where some speech functions are reinforced, deviated, or inhibited. All mechanisms are interrelated and, through association and feedback loops, combine to produce learning. The motor speech area is on the left side of the frontal lobe for right-handed persons; other areas occupy both right and left regions of the cerebrum; the hearing association area in the temporal lobe; the visual speech center in the occipital lobe; and the written speech area in an extension forward from the motor cortex, located above the motor speech area in the frontal lobe.

Other gross structures

THALAMUS AND HYPOTHALAMUS. Two vital structures maintain a sentinal position in the central section of the brain. The thalamus acts as a relay center, monitoring sensory stimuli, suppressing some and magnifying others. The hypothalamus, located midline and below the thalamus, contains cells that control body temperature, water balance, sleep, appetite, and some spontaneous emotions such as fear and pleasure. Both divisions of the autonomic nervous system are under the control of the hypothalamus.

MIDBRAIN. The midbrain forms one of the forward parts of the brain stem. Four rounded masses of gray matter, hidden by the cerebral hemispheres, comprise the corpora quadrigemina and act as relay centers for certain eye and ear reflexes. The ventral white matter contains fibers that conduct impulses between centers in the cerebrum and lower centers in the pons, cerebellum, medulla, and spinal cord. The midbrain is in a strategic position to receive a major output of the limbic system as well as impulses from the hypothalamus (Moore, 1973).

CEREBELLUM. Like the cerebral cortex, the cerebellum has an outer layer of gray matter and an inner portion largely of white matter. It consists of two lateral hemispheres and a narrow medial portion, the vermis. Three bundles of nerve fibers connect the cerebellum to the brain stem and, through it, to other parts of the nervous system. The bundles are called peduncles: the inferior, middle, and superior.

The cerebellum serves to modulate and regulate impulses, receiving information from and sending messages back to the vestibular nuclei. It gathers input from general proprioceptors and cutaneous sense organs, processes it, and influences neural activity down the spinal cord and upward through routes to the cortex. At the higher levels it influences coordination required in complicated or skillful muscular movements.

The cerebellum is responsible for muscle synergy: It "times" contractions of muscle. Voluntary movement can proceed without assistance from the cerebellum but is clumsy and disorganized, a dysfunction called cerebellar ataxia.

PONS. The pons (bridge) is made up largely of nerve fibers that carry messages from one side of the cerebellum to the other side, from the cerebellum to the cerebrum and midbrain, and from the cerebellum to lower centers in the medulla and spinal cord. It thus serves as an important link between the cerebellum and the rest of the nervous system. The largest component of the reticular system resides here and in the medulla.

The pons also contains connections with the trigeminal nerve (fifth cranial nerve), the abducent nerve (sixth cranial nerve), the facial nerve (seventh cranial nerve), and the acoustic nerve (eighth cranial nerve).

MEDULLA OBLONGATA. The medulla oblongata contains collections of cell bodies, or nuclei, including ones of the glossopharyngeal (ninth cranial nerve), the vagus (tenth cranial nerve), the accessory (eleventh cranial nerve), and the hypoglossal (twelfth cranial nerve). Thus the medulla is the site of vital centers to the organism: the respiratory center, cardiac center, and vasomotor center. Among the reflexes controlled in the medulla are the salivary-taste reflex, carotid body reflex, cough reflex, gag reflex, and vomiting reflex.

Fibers passing through the medulla may decussate, or cross over. This shifting results in the right cerebral hemisphere controlling the left side of the body, and the left hemisphere the right side.

Structure of the spinal cord. The spinal cord has two major functions: It integrates reflex behavior that occurs in the trunk and limbs, and it conducts nervous impulses to and from the brain. The spinal cord descends from the medulla oblongata to the region of the first lumbar vertebra, where it ends in a tapered cone. When viewed in a transverse section, the cord shows a small irregular, butterfly-shaped internal section made up of gray matter that is unmyelinated nerve bodies. White matter surrounding the gray portion is made up of thousands of myelinated nerve fibers.

Spinal nerves are attached to the cord in pairs: eight cervical, twelve thoracic, five lumbar, five sacral, and one coccygeal. Each spinal nerve, as we have learned, has dorsal and ventral roots that form nearly continuous rows along the cord. In addition to mediating skeletal muscle, the spinal cord is connected, through special nerves branching off from it, to the autonomic nervous system. The sympathetic branch lies along the middle region of the cord and consists of a chain of ganglia that send out a diffuse network of fibers to the organs innervated by it. Fibers of the parasympathetic branch arise from the hindmost region of the cord and the brain. As mentioned earlier, the parasympathetic system responds locally rather than generally so that its fibers go directly to the individual organs it innervates.

It should be noted that in the region of the limbs, spinal nerves regroup to form a network of nerves called the plexus and comprise the cervical, brachial, and lumbosacral plexuses.

There are many connections occurring within the spinal cord. Integration taking place at this level serves to organize various sensory information so that patterns are set up in the motor neurons. This kind of integration contributes and leads to organized response patterns reflected in the behavioral motor responses seen during an activities of daily living assessment.

CONCLUSION

We have come full circle: from the initiation of sensations by receptors, to their integration in the central nervous system, to the sensory impressions or motor responses that follow. Our purpose in this review has been to renew an understanding of behavior that results from collective activity in the nervous system. Before proceeding to correlate the information contained in the review with what may be observed in an assessment, some brief conclusions should be summarized:

- Information in the form of an impulse is gathered by sensory receptors and inhibited or facilitated at synapses along the neuron chain; these synapses are located at various levels in the central nervous system.
- Protective responses take precedence.
- Sensory modalities, at work simultaneously, reinforce each other in providing sensory impressions.
- Sensory and motor systems modulate each other through feedback loops.
- Higher levels of the central nervous system do not function optimally without adequate lower function.
- The cerebral cortex, although it exerts a commanding role, must operate in conjunction with the older nervous system.
- There is a hierarchical order of integration.
- The brain responds as a whole, a united network.
- The reticular activating system serves to keep the brain active and the organism alert.
- The motor system maintains a background of posture and tone against which fine discrete phasic movements are carried out.
- The autonomic system controls visceral and endocrine activities.
- Associational systems correlate received sensory stimuli with past experience and impose an influence over inhibitory and excitatory activity at the synapses, leading to an organized execution of behavior through motor pathways.

PART II

Relationship of neuromotor, sensorimotor, and perceptual-motor development to self-care function

NEONATAL STIMULATION

During the last decade many ideas on the sensory needs of humans have been emerging and coalescing. Some of these ideas are now incorporated into programs of health care, with increased attention focused on sensory input during the early stages of life. Researchers, looking back to "prenatal" influences, point to the rich intrauterine environment with its varied and continuous sensations—auditory stimuli from the mother's heartbeat, tactile, kinesthetic, and vestibular stimuli from the structures of the womb, the mother's movements, or the movements of the fetus. There is concern that after birth, stimuli may be increased in type and intensity beyond what is comfortable for the newborn or, at the opposite extreme, decrease below his need for stimulation.

Views about the responsiveness of the newborn infant are changing as the result of scientific observations. Brazelton (1973) has made a special study of the newborn's reactions to stimuli and concludes that the newborn infant has the capacity to shape his environment. Contrary to concepts about infant behavior held during the second quarter of this century, new data indicate that the infant exerts measures of control over his environment and that, in fact, he can screen out and protect himself from stimuli, can initiate activity, adapt behavior, sense his needs, try to communicate them, and even quiet and console himself (Erickson, 1976).

As a part of his studies, Brazelton (1973) devised The Neonatal Assessment Scale, which measures the infant's inherent neurological capacities and his responses to certain sets of stimuli. Through its use parent-infant interaction potentially becomes predictable. Findings derived from the assessment enable professionals to offer parents individualized information about infant care—when it is most optimal to present stimuli to a particular baby, when to refrain from stimulation, when to console, and so on, based on the baby's uniqueness in responding as identified by the assessment results. Sensory information is thus becoming increasingly specific for the individual.

The discussion in this chapter remains a general one, based on broad patterns of maturation within which each child displays his own developmental rate and style. Ideas about neuromotor, sensory, and perceptual growth are combined to give a chronological account of events that ultimately affect self-care function.

EXTEROCEPTORS—THE SENSORY EXPLORERS

It is with his hands that man most frequently reaches out to explore his environment—its textures, temperatures, contours, flexibility, sizes, and weights. Tactile information enhances visual impressions.

At birth the infant's gaze is inconsistent, but beginning in the second month of life he can regularly converge on and focus on near objects. He begins to notice his hands, usually the extended hand in the preferred tonic neck reflex posture. During the third and fourth month sustained hand regard continues, and by 5 months of age the infant begins to coordinate vision and manipulation. His new skill of grasping is visually directed. As Ayres (1958) accurately puts it, "Much of the purposeful movements of the hands become so because the eyes have observed and directed them as such." Often the infant takes objects to his mouth, to explore their properties with his tongue and lips, which together with the hands have a large number of neurons terminating in the sensory cortex. By 10 months of age sustained attention with the eyes is no longer required for reaching tasks. The infant can now visually appraise the movement needed for reaching before initiating the act.

Touch is a predominant sensation at birth, although not refined. It is tactile stimuli that elicit the rooting reflex which is helpful to the baby in locating his source of food. However, he lacks the capacity to generate tactile stimulation fully because of the immaturity of his visual system, his lack of grasp, and the strong avoidance responses rapidly initiated by him. Typically the newborn infant withdraws his feet and extends and spreads his fingers, thus preventing sustained contact with his environment. These responses are global, undifferentiated, and directed toward self-protection. Stockmeyer (1972) notes that the distal parts of the body have a high concentration of rapidly adapting receptors. According to her, these receptors are possibly the same ones involved in discriminating functions that develop later. Discrete tactile sense occurs after modification of withdrawal patterns, when advanced motor functions also emerge such as voluntary grasping.

Tactile stimulation must be enlarged on by caregivers during the neonatal period, and indeed, nurturing rituals throughout the world's cultures include touching—caressing, holding, and kissing. As the baby becomes more comfortable with being touched, moved, and manipulated, he begins to understand that the physical contact is limited to a specific area of his body (Hayes and Komick, 1971). Tactile sense begins to function in a more precise manner. The infant's capacity to explore, initiate, and sustain contact with his environment increases then at the fourth to fifth month, when his tactile system is becoming more discriminatory, his vision is sufficiently coordinated to monitor reaching movements, and his hands come together for clasping.

Frequently, a mothering figure talks to a baby or sings, creating sound waves that stimulate exteroceptors in the inner ear. Forms of stimuli—tactile, visual, and acoustic—are believed to be essential for the infant's growth processes to occur. For example, studies have shown that deprivation of tactile stimuli leads to emotional and perceptual abnormalities. One existing concept looks on the skin, with its many tactile receptors, as the literal boundary between self and non-self. In such a context it can be viewed as a facilitator to the establishment of an individual's self-concept.

PROPRIOCEPTORS—LEARNING ABOUT SPACE

A caregiver may soothe a baby through rocking, a source of vestibular stimulation. Later, at 6 months of age, self-generated vestibular stimulation is available to the infant through his emerging skill to deliberately roll. This stimulation is often vigorous, and the period of practice precedes voluntary sitting, which requires first and foremost the orientation of the head in space through the help of receptors in the semicircular canals. Rolling also provides increased stimulation to touch and pressure receptors of the trunk and limbs and to proprioceptors of neck musculature.

That movement provides sensory stimulation to proprioceptors in muscles, tendons, and joints, which, in turn, contribute to the formation of a body scheme has been suggested previously through references to Ayres, Head, Rosen, Knickerbocker. Ayres (1972) also suggests that praxis, the ability to motor plan, may be more dependent on the joint receptors, whereas posture may be more related to receptors in the muscle spindle. Some observations are now presented that call attention to motor behaviors preceding advanced motility.

Joint approximation is seen at 3 months as the baby begins to develop propping reactions in the prone position. This occurs first primarily at the shoulders and later extends to the elbows, wrists, and fingers, when at 8 months, lying on his stomach, he raises the upper part of his body from the surface on which he rests. By 10 months the baby attains the sitting position from prone by using a ventral push, and this increases the quantity of stimuli to joint receptors throughout his upper extremities. He also begins to crawl, pulling himself along with his arms. Between 2 and 5 years his pattern of coming to a sitting position is characterized by partial rotation. Joint approximation decreases in this activity until finally, by 5 years, with the integration of the body righting (on the body) reaction, he comes to a sitting position symmetrically without necessarily supporting himself.

Vigorous joint approximation occurs in the lower extremities prior to walking as the child pulls himself up at the rail of his playpen and bounces up and down joyously and repeatedly. These patterns of motor action tend to suggest that there may be a period of self-generated, repetitious stimulation, a kind of preparatory period, prior to acquisition of more skilled, planned motor acts. When movement becomes automatic and refined, the quantity of self-induced stimulation appears to decrease.

MORE ABOUT MOTOR PLANNING

Basic motor acts such as feeding oneself, particularly manipulating utensils, do not occur automatically but are learned. When first initiated, the child has a conscious awareness of movement; he visually monitors progression of his plan, and he repeats the movement sequences again and again, gradually modifying and refining them, both in timing and efficiency.

A part of his motor planning includes carrying out acts of assumption, as described by Voss (1972). For example, planning involves positioning his hands for work in such a way that movement is promoted. A classical example is a child learning to use scissors. His task is twofold: he must sequence and combine appropriate patterns of movement (motor planning), while at the same time making compensatory adjustments in body posture to maintain postural stability (postural control).

Combined sensory systems—tactile, kinesthetic, and visual—are activated as the child performs deliberate motor acts and utilizes his internal postural model, or body scheme. His early attempts at new motor acts are characterized by exploration, experimentation, trial and error, or imitation.

Consider the feeding sequence. When the child first feeds himself finger foods, he examines food particles with his hands, intently studying his pincer grasp of crumbs before bringing the tiny pieces to his mouth. He does not always regulate the force of his grip, and crackers easily break. Early attempts to use a spoon are considerably more difficult and even more experimental. At 1 year of age there is poor filling because he is unsure of how to manipulate the spoon, to make it an extension of his own body movement. Not infrequently, he turns the spoon upside down before it enters his mouth. He is also likely to turn it in his mouth. It is not until his third year that he relinquishes his palmar grasp and begins to hold the spoon with his fingers. Some time later he incorporates supination as a part of the plate-to-mouth pattern.

Motor acts frequently require the use of both sides of the body in a coordinated way and may necessitate crossing the midline of the body. Neurological bilateral integration then occurs at various cortical and subcortical levels so that, for example, the child may know what each hand is doing. Cutting meat with a knife in one hand while stabilizing the meat with a fork in the other hand is a complex feat and is seldom accomplished until approximately 7 years of age.

Incumbent in the process of integration are some spatial ideas, which precede verbal identification; that is, the child must be aware of the two sides of his body and their interrelationship, a function referred to as *laterality*, even though he may be unable to label the sides as "right" or "left" until around 7 years of age. Having developed the spatial idea of laterality, he next gains a sense of *directionality*, an awareness of directions in external space.

Motor planning can be summarized as "knowing how to give the body precise directions" (Ayres, 1958). It continues throughout life whenever an individual is faced with a new motor task—the execution of a new dance step, assuming a new yoga position, and so on. But once the movements become automatic, are successful and memorized for recall, conscious motor planning is no longer needed. The demands for planning movement cease.

VISUAL SPATIAL DEVELOPMENT

The close working relationship of vision with other sensory systems has been duly emphasized. Because they so mutually reinforce each other, impressions gained by one system stimulate associations and recall of those from other systems. An example of this is manual *stereognosis*, the ability to recognize the form of a solid object by touch. As an individual visually appraises an object, his hand feels the surface while spatial qualities are conveyed by proprioceptive and cutaneous impulses resulting from position, movement, and contact (Ayres, 1958). Later, visual cues alone cause recall of these manual impressions, or it is the manual impressions that stimulate the visual associations. Many other examples have been cited previously that illustrate the close ties of vision, tactile, and proprioceptive modalities in contributing to the formation of spatial perceptions and concepts.

Visual appraisal begins with the ability to attend, focus, and follow with the eyes. But before an object can be seen, its image must be projected on the retina and the resultant impulses transferred to the visual cortex (Ayres, 1958). When an individual looks at an object or scene, the view seen by the right eye is slightly different from the view seen by the left eye. These two dissimilar retinal images are fused in the visual cortex to give a three-dimensional picture having depth as well as height and width. According to Watson and Lowrey (1967), depth sense is developed as the visual acuity grows sharper, as ocular muscles become coordinated, and as the brain learns to fuse images. Some investigators believe this occurs at approximately 6 years of age. Other factors contribute to recognition of solidity, depth, and distance, namely, relative brightness, clearness, and color. In addition to perspective effects, the intensity of these qualities defines edges of objects, reflects texture of surface, and distinguishes figure from background (Ayres, 1958).

The sequence for visual appraisal is that the infant first recognizes the nearness of objects, then sees two close objects as separate, and next becomes aware that objects are the same under different spatial relations (Ayres, 1958). In the process of viewing he learns to separate foreground from background. As his visual exploration proceeds, perception is quickly altered, since as the focus of the eyes shift, that which is the center of attention becomes the foreground and the surrounding area the background. Having perceived the object as a whole, the infant's next task is to recognize its form and establish associations leading to concepts and identification. Relative size and shape are additional pieces of information to be incorporated.

The developmental process becomes clearer when we consider the child's growth in functional tasks as outlined by Gesell and others and noted by Ayres. As early as 4 months of age the baby recognizes the form of his bottle, if he is bottle fed, and opens his mouth adaptively. At 7 to 10 months he can use geometrical form discrimination as a learning cue, and at 1½ years he places a round object in a round hole. He begins to name colors, although seldom correctly, but by 3 years he can match red and yellow. Before he points to a familiar object in a picture, he participates in motor tasks of identification; for example, he imitates gestures involving an object at 1½ years, then points to an object according to function at 2 years, and finally recognizes familiar objects in pictures at 2½ years (Brown, 1974).

Additionally, Ayres (1958) states that at 2½ years the child becomes aware of the important dualisms of up and down, in and out, back and forth, top and bottom, back and front, high and low, near and far. Verbal labels are gradually attached, and by 4½ years a child correctly locates above, below, and behind (Brown, 1974). Ayres further describes that spatial relations are first mastered in the immediate area—"mouth space," "visual space," and "tactile space"—then gradually extend out and away from the individual. By 4 years of age a child can sense height, width, and depth simultaneously.

Visual-spatial percepts become more structured and recognizable when forms are reproduced, which involves a combination of vision and motor. As early as 1 year, a child may make incidental marks with a crayon or pencil, followed by scribbles that may go off the page. Later, he imitates a vertical line, followed by a horizontal line, and by 3 or 4 years can copy a circle. As his repertory continues to enlarge, he combines a vertical and horizontal line to copy a cross and, at 6 years, joins four lines to form a square. Finally, he succeeds in printing a few letters of the alphabet. By 8 years he can print between lines and at 8½ years writes his name in cursive, a more demanding motor planning task.

SIGNALS OF DYSFUNCTION TO BE NOTED DURING AN ACTIVITIES OF DAILY LIVING ASSESSMENT

Perceptual dysfunction may result from defects in receiving stimuli and poor neural organization in processing stimuli. The result is that environmental stimuli, external and internal, may be perceived inaccurately or acted on in an inefficient, inappropriate way.

During an activities of daily living assessment, probably the most obvious signals of poor sensory reception and neural integration that result in perceptual dysfunction appear in the subtest of written communication. The signs are not limited to the difficulty of graphic reproduction alone but also to the child's assumed posture, the way he positions his hand, his grip on the pencil, the rotation (or lack of it) of the paper on which he writes, the stabilization of the paper with the other hand, the degree to which the eyes follow his hand at work, his use of the paper's space, the proximity of eyes to hands, and the transfer of pencil from hand to hand, particularly if associated with crossing the midline.

Signals of dysfunction in other activities are not as clear cut, but in dressing there are characteristic clues. These include the way the child positions himself for work, the way he sequences movement such as in lacing and tying, his spatial discrimination in distinguishing the sides of his body, his identification of body parts, his awareness of where his limbs are in space, his understanding of spatial concepts, and his attentiveness in visually monitoring body movements. Awkwardness and poor sequencing suggest the possibility of difficulty with praxis. Further evidence may be demonstrated in the use of tools such as eating utensils.

Problems in recognizing form, combined with a poor body scheme, may prevent the child from identifying the right shoe from the left or placing the shoe on the correct foot, a skill that should be accomplished by about 4 years of age.

More subtle signs of difficulty during an assessment involve avoiding crossing the midline of the body such as in lacing shoes or combing and parting the hair. A child may also tend to ignore an extremity or side of his body.

Finally, behaviors that may have relevance include sensitivity to being touched, hyperactivity, distractibility, failure to locate objects in his surroundings, and emotional lability.

None of these signals can be considered diagnostic because perceptual function is too complex to be identified problematically on the basis of observation alone. Sufficient quantity of signs should alert the assessor of the need for further investigation through specific diagnostic procedures.

REFERENCES

Ayres, A. J. 1958. The visual-motor function. Am. J. Occup. Ther. **12:**130-138.
Ayres, A. J. 1964. Perceptual-motor dysfunction in children. Ohio Occupational Therapy Association Conference, Cincinnati, Greater Cincinnati District (a monograph).
Ayres, A. J. 1972. Sensory integration and learning disorders. Los Angeles, Western Psychological Services.
Bobath, K. 1966. The motor deficit in patients with cerebral palsy. London, William Heinemann, Ltd.
Brazelton, T. B. 1973. The neonatal behavioral assessment scale. Philadelphia, J. B. Lippincott Co.
Brown, C. B. 1974. Functional developmental assessment. Palo Alto, Calif., Children's Hospital at Stanford.
Dethier, V. G., and Stellar, E. 1970. Animal behavior, ed. 3. Englewood Cliffs, N.J., Prentice-Hall, Inc.
Erickson, M. L. 1976. Assessment and management of developmental changes in children. St. Louis, The C. V. Mosby Co.
Frostig, M., and Maslow, P. 1970. Movement education—theory and practice. Chicago, Follett Publishing Co.

Gatz, A. J. 1973. Manter's essentials of clinical neuroanatomy and neurophysiology, ed. 4. Philadelphia, F. A. Davis Co.

Gotten, N., and Wilson, L. 1949. Neurologic nursing, ed. 2. Philadelphia, F. A. Davis Co.

Hayes, M., and Komick, M. P. 1971. The development of visual-perceptual-motor function. In Banus, B. S.: The developmental therapist. Thorofare, N.J., Charles B. Slack, Inc.

Hilgard, E. R., and Bower, G. H. 1975. Theories of learning, ed. 4. Englewood Cliffs, N.J., Prentice-Hall, Inc.

Huss, A. J. 1971. Sensorimotor treatment approaches. In Willard, H. S., and Spackman, C. S., editors: Occupational therapy, ed. 4. Philadelphia, J. B. Lippincott Co.

Knickerbocker, B. M. 1966. The significance of body scheme and body image in perceptual-motor dysfunction. Proceedings of Ohio Occupational Therapy Association Conference on Body Image, Cleveland.

Moore, J. C. 1973. Sensorimotor integration, a workshop. San Diego, University of California Extension.

Moore, J. C. 1976. Behavior, bias, and the limbic system. The Eleanor Clarke Slagle Lecture. Am. J. Occup. Ther. 30:11-19.

Mueller, C. 1965. Sensory psychology. Englewood Cliffs, N.J., Prentice-Hall, Inc.

Rosen, I. M. 1966. Development of body image. Proceedings of Ohio Occupational Therapy Association Conference on Body Image, Cleveland.

Stockmeyer, S. A. 1972. Sensorimotor approach to treatment. In Pearson, P. H., and Williams, C. E., editors: Physical therapy services in the developmental disabiliites. Springfield, Ill., Charles C Thomas, Publisher.

Van Allen, M. W. 1969. Pictorial manual of neurologic tests. Chicago, Year Book Medical Publishers, Inc.

Voss, D. E. 1972. Proprioceptive neuromuscular facilitation—the pnf method. In Pearson, P. H., and Williams, C. E., editors: Physical therapy services in the developmental disabilities. Springfield, Ill., Charles C Thomas, Publisher.

Watson, E. H., and Lowrey, G. H. 1967. Growth and development of children, ed. 5. Chicago, Year Book Medical Publishers, Inc.

Wyke, B. 1975. The neurological basis of movement—a developmental review. In Holt, K. S., editor: Movement and child development. Philadelphia, J. B. Lippincott Co.

Zoethout, W. D., and Tuttle, W. W. 1958. Textbook of physiology, ed. 13. St. Louis, The C. V. Mosby Co.

8 Implications of cognitive function

There are two important reasons for an assessor to understand how cognitive skill develops in a child. The first reason is so that he can detect subtle adaptive responses in the child's performance, and the second pertains to his own performance as an assessor and teacher. Teaching requires an ability to analyze and structure tasks, calibrating their demands from an intellectual standpoint. The assessor, as a teacher, determines what the child knows concerning the task and, to some extent, how he knows it. He identifies those sensory modalities and cognitive skills that the child utilizes in activating his plan of action. When necessary, the assessor interrupts and sequences steps making up the task.

STAGES OF COGNITIVE DEVELOPMENT

Cognition refers to the intellectual activities of the mind and includes mental acts such as perceiving, discriminating, associating, remembering, reasoning, comprehending, and generalizing.

Sensory motor exploration

The early stages of cognitive development have already been examined, since its roots begin in early neuromotor maturation. The primitive reflexes of infancy that are innate and have a stimulus-bound quality provide posture and movement, which the child practices. New patterns of movement and response are sequentially formed and relationships established through repetition, trial and error, and reinforcement, a form of conditioning. The child acquires a repertory of movement patterns, which he organizes around certain functions such as reaching, rolling over, and coming to sitting from the prone position. Gradually he progresses from movement patterns to selective and varied movement. Through movement he explores his environment, gathering information through sensory input: auditory, visual, tactile, and kinesthetic.

Perceptual manipulations

With increased awareness the child notes consequences of outgoing responses and incoming sensory information. He becomes aware of similarities, differences, and results. With the establishment of a body of perceptual information, he can internalize his experiential information so that overt motor manipulations are not necessarily required. Chaney and Kephart (1968) explain: "Overt motor manipulations are necessary only as confirmatory data when the perceptual event is complex and unclear."*

With the ability to process perceptual data and assign meaning to sensory impressions and motor actions, the child begins to note and deal with symbolic material. For example, he can look at a picture and vicariously experience a visual message. He can, in effect, form mental images of his own, and through imagery he can relate his perceptions to previous perceptual experience. Moreover, through the acquisition of speech he can enter into a sharing process with others. This greatly enlarges the possibility for increasing his overall body of knowledge through a new mode of interaction.

Language—a learned skill

In the definition of Battin and Haug (1970), "Language is every form of communication in which thoughts and feelings are symbolized."† This includes facial expression, gestures, pantomine, speech, writing, and even expression through art. Battin and Haug explain that speech represents one form of language in which symbols, in the form of sounds or words, are used to convey thoughts.

In a broad sense an infant's cry is a kind of language in that it is a means of obtaining attention and represents a limited way of controlling the environment. When comforted by a caregiver, an infant does not understand the words spoken, but he does experience a kind of conditioning by the emotional tone of the caregiver's voice. Such auditory experiences lay the groundwork for comprehension.

Increasingly, the infant "tunes in" to a world of sound, including his own voice. His coos and babblings are repeated with varying intensity and loudness. They are sounds without meaning but are vital to language formation. In fact, the infant will understand speech long before using it. Initially, his word association is not exacting, and there is a more or less loose connection between sounds and a state of being.

A child's first words become true speech when he uses them to designate a specific object (Battin and Haug, 1970). Words are then functional and serve a purpose. They are used intentionally and deliberately to exert a measure of control. Inner language, the aspect that permits a word to have meaning, is basic to verbal expression and is referred to as *basic concept formation.*

Words assist the child in refining interactions with his environment. Verbalization becomes a "time-saver," a means of increasing efficiency (Beadle, 1976). Moreover, with verbal expression there is less need to explore the environment. As noted previously, speech becomes a regulatory mechanism over social behavior, enhancing

*From Chaney, C. M., and Kephart, N. C. 1968. Motoric aids to perceptual training, p. 21. Columbus, Charles E. Merrill Publishing Co.
†From Battin, R. R., and Haug, C. O.: Speech and language delay—a home training program, p. 3. Springfield, Ill., 1970, Charles C Thomas, Publisher.

the formation of social schemes and helping to sublimate strong drives. For example, behavior can be classified verbally for the child according to "cans" and "cannots." "You can throw a ball outside. You cannot throw a ball in the house." "You can run in the yard. You cannot run into the street." Language and, most importantly, speech enable the child to code his experiences (Luria, 1960).

Speech has to be a shared system. Implicit in its use is the sharing of thoughts, wants, and needs between one individual and another (Beadle, 1976). It must be functional, serving as a communication link between the child and those around him, and, it should be noted, speech does not occur automatically but is acquired through imitation and practice. Used purposefully, it is an important means of focusing attention, a requirement for learning. Language helps the child to advance his function from the intuitive level, based on direct experience and immediate perception, to the next state of reason and logic.

Cognition—concrete and formal operations

Piaget uses the term *operations* for activities of the mind as opposed to the bodily activities of the sensorimotor period (Pulaski, 1971), but there is a blending between the two stages. It is through extensive manipulations of the environment with its objects that a child structures reality and organizes his observations. Through comparisons he categorizes perceptions into series, classes, numbers, clusters, and groups. Perception provides information; cognition permits the child to decode it and make matches and inferences. From the initial perceptions he organizes abstract relationships, leading to concepts. Chaney and Kephart (1968) state: "These concepts can then be manipulated and combined into more and more abstract concepts in which the perceptual basis is less and less apparent."* Pulaski's study of Piaget's theories of cognitive development lead her to describe this phenomenon as the child "being freed from the pull of immediate perception." This freedom permits him to range mentally forward and backward in space and time. Pulaski, interpreting Piaget's ideas, points out that this speeds up the thinking process considerably and gives it much greater mobility and freedom. The mind can reverse its activity and coordinate previous experience with present circumstances. In spite of this new freedom, however, the child is capable only of thought about concrete, existing objects and people. He understands the relationship of classes and can put objects and events in serial order, but he cannot make deductions from a hypothesis, a tentative theory, or a supposition. This level of thought ordinarily will not be attainable until his adolescent years, at a stage Piaget labels *formal operations*.

Piaget uses various terms to describe processes familiar among learning theories under other names. Included among the terms is *equilibration*, which refers to maintaining a state of internal balance. Piaget views equilibration as being dependent on the sum of experience in learning to adjust to both physical and social worlds. Such

---

*From Chaney, C. M., and Kephart, N. C. 1968. Motoric aids to perceptual training, p. 22. Columbus, Charles E. Merrill Publishing Co.

an adaptation process is continuous throughout life. The individual absorbs all forms of information and reintegrates them into existing mental structures or schemas, a process that Piaget calls *assimilation.* The modification that occurs simultaneously, whereby the individual alters patterns of behavior to cope with the new information, is described as *accommodation.* According to Piaget, mental function, the acquisition of knowledge and competence, is a consequence of growth, biological maturation, and an individual's interaction with his physical and social environment (Hilgard and Bower, 1975). This view has implications for interpreting psychological tests, which will be commented on as the discussion progresses.

MEASURING MENTAL FUNCTION

A clinical psychologist fills the important role of defining a child's potential—his strengths and weaknesses. An assessment of perceptual and cognitive function is carried out through psychometric testing, procedures that have evolved from the mental testing movement at the turn of the century.

Psychometric tests represent a standardized assessment as described by Banus (1971). The tests are highly structured with strict procedures as to presentation, timing, and scoring, and normative data are used for evaluating the performance.

A psychologist is a valuable consultant to an assessor of self-care in a number of ways. Objective, measured psychological data contribute to the validation of the assessor's perceptions of behavior. Additionally, through professional training and ability to interpret, a psychologist can make prognosticating statements that have implications for the child's future performance in activities of daily living.

Therapists can also benefit by familiarizing themselves with psychometric test items. Among the most reliable intelligence scales used today are the Stanford-Binet, the Wechsler Intelligence Scale for Children (WISC), and the Wechsler Preschool and Primary Scale of Intelligence (WPPSI). Other tests individually administered include the Peabody Picture Vocabulary Test, the Columbia Mental Maturity Scale, and the Leiter International Performance Scale. Of these various tests, the Stanford-Binet is of special interest for this discussion because an analysis of the age levels for which the Stanford-Binet subtests are constructed in effect gives an outline of cognitive development. It may offer the reader a more illustrative way of viewing such growth. Through examining the requirements for tasks, one can begin to recognize relationships between the level of demand and the mechanisms utilized in making a successful response.

Organization of intellectual tasks

In 1965, Sattler (1974) presented a classification scheme for the 1960 Stanford-Binet test using seven categories: language, memory, conceptual thinking, reasoning, numerical reasoning, visual-motor, and social intelligence. He described function in these categories at three levels, early year level, middle year level, and adolescent year level, which bear similarities to the stages of perceptual manipulations and cognitive operations at concrete and formal stages. The tasks presented at the various levels trace progression in problem solving from simple trial-and-error solution to the employment of symbolic processes. The following description incorporates Sattler's "Developmental Analysis of Intelligence."*

Early year level

Psychological tests for the 2- through 5-year-old child involve visual-motor tasks such as block building, stringing beads, and copying a circle or straight line. Block play reveals the child's ability to imitate, to construct a model from memory, or to copy. It permits many observations on general behavior, motor ability, spatial relations, and the child's ability or desire to imitate or experiment.

Language development is assessed through the child's knowledge of common objects found in his environment. The stimuli are perceptual, and definitions may be given by a related word, illustrating his formation of simple concepts.

Knowledge of the social world is measured by the child's understanding of pictures and knowing the functions of the objects presented.

Middle year level

Memory ability increases with maturation and test items reflect this. The child is required to perform more complex tasks from simple repetition of digits, a preschool task, to repeating digits backward, a mental exercise that measures auditory short-term memory. The reproduction of designs tests visual memory.

Visual-motor tasks are still included, but they are less numerous. Copying a diamond, paper cutting, and maze tracing represent more complex visual analysis and ability to motor plan.

During the middle years a child acquires the ability to do arithmetic calculations, and standard operations consist of addition, subtraction, multiplication, and division. At a later stage when he approaches adolescence, the child is challenged by complex symbol manipulation that involves spatial reasoning. Attention, concentration, memory, and prior learning all contribute to success in performing.

Language ability is now tested by verbal stimuli rather than perceptual representations, and phrase responses are no longer adequate. The child is required to give increasingly complex verbal descriptions and definitions. Many tasks relating to language also reflect his reasoning ability. The child is asked to apply language to rhyming, defining abstract words, making word combinations, and building sentences.

Adolescent level

Verbal reasoning is a prominent feature of cognitive function in the adolescent, who is expected to have some appreciation for "abstract subtleties" of his culture. Verbal absurdities are introduced to challenge his reasoning capacity. Another subtest measures his understanding of proverbs, which requires well-developed reasoning, verbal comprehension, analysis, and generalization.

*Modified from Sattler, J. M. 1974. Assessment of children's intelligence, pp. 134-138. Philadelphia, W. B. Saunders Co.

Memory function is tested through recall of more difficult perceptual material, by orally presented digits, and by longer and more complex sentences.

Demands of intellectual tasks

When the psychologist compiles test results, one of the aspects he examines is the pattern of performance, the areas of strength and weakness, and the scattering of scores. He considers the demands of the tasks from several views. Higher cognitive functions require imagery, memory, judgment, critical evaluation, and problem solving (Frostig and Maslow, 1970). Tasks may also be broken down according to verbal or nonverbal skills, concrete or abstract reasoning, and long-term or short-term memory. Tasks may require various cognitive functions but may predominantly call for a single one such as comprehension, judgment, or practical information.

Overt behavioral traits may have special significance: the kind of attention the child gives to the task, his regard for detail or whole, signs of impulsiveness, or involved concentration. Such signs reflect his ability to screen out stimuli, to discriminate, and to organize perceptions.

There are numerous and complex details to be sifted, an essential part of the process that enables the psychologist to make interpretations. Some significant observations may be detected by various disciplinary members, including the psychologist, social worker, physical therapist, teacher, nurse, and assessor of a self-care performance. These will be described shortly.

In making conclusions a psychologist considers the child's previous experiences, his cultural opportunities, his interest patterns, and his motivation—those interactions with his environment specified by Piaget. He notes those qualities of performance which make the child unique. In addition, he considers a time frame. Taylor (1971) makes the point that a child presents variations, but in general, efficiency in tasks increases with age as he becomes more proficient in organizing clues and utilizes present and past experience. Particular abilities may be called on more frequently at one age than another. Taylor describes a brain-injured child who excelled in verbal facility and superficial social skills during childhood, although he had considerable difficulty in reasoning and learning. These deficits were less apparent at the earlier stages of development because the demands on his reasoning powers were not dominant. However, in adolescence the inability to perceive the subtleties in the environment and poor social judgment inhibit relationships with others. Taylor (1971) explains: "To families and outsiders, some children may appear to deteriorate, since they seem less well off than they were in their earlier, 'brighter' years. In reality, their endowment has not changed for the worse; it is simply that the skills which were effective then no longer suffice. Disabilities which were present but relatively unobtrusive in early years become a true hindrance later on."* Difficulties can be foreseen, but caution and restraint are always desirable in making predictions

*From Taylor, E. M. 1971. Psychological appraisal of children with cerebral defects, p. 223. Cambridge, Mass., Harvard University Press.

for the individual child. Taylor's case illustrations are examples of how developmental tasks require different coping skills at various periods in life.

OBSERVATIONS DURING AN ACTIVITIES OF DAILY LIVING ASSESSMENT
In use of language

Significantly, language skills are positively correlated with the intellectual ability to reason. Sattler (1974) describes a child's use of language as a guide to both his thought processes and personality style. Problems related to mental function can be detected by the manner in which the child speaks, his vocabulary, and the content of his verbalizations.

Examples of language distortions include circumlocution, verbal perseveration, incomplete thoughts, blocking, word searching, illogical reasoning, irrelevant details, and automatic phrases. Emotional regression, rigidity, denial, and depression reflect emotional states; laughter may be exhibited, not as an expression of joy but rather as a release of tension. A child's responses may show a discrepancy between receptive and expressive language abilities.

In motor responses

An assessor also notes motor components of a task, which are detailed elsewhere in the handbook. Beyond obvious signs of weakness, tremor, or other incoordination, there may be subtle dysfunction, involving the child's ability to organize a motor task and carry out the steps in an orderly sequence.

In use of sensory modalities

As the child gathers sensory information, he may show a preferential use of a sensory modality, for example, sight, hearing, or touch, which becomes evident in his interactions with people and objects. For example, an assessor may note whether the child "looks" selectively and has visual interest in people, in their activities and interactions, in objects, and in furnishings. He may observe if the child readily orients himself to sound, whether he predominantly uses speech, or if his means of expression tend to be through manual or facial gesture or both.

The degree with which he visually and auditorally attends may point toward a strength or weakness that affects function. Auditory recall, or verbal imagery, is necessary for speech, and visual sequencing is important in spelling, reading, and arithmetic. Being aware of the child's ability to process visually and auditorally is important in presenting tasks to the child so that the number of auditory or visual directions do not exceed his ability for recall. Other aspects of auditory and visual memory and sequencing are concerned with the ability to perceive details, not just the order in which the child sees or hears. He must separate out foreground from background, recognize the whole as well as parts to the whole, and organize his perceptions.

An assessor may note the child's tendency to touch and manipulate objects before proceeding with a task. His method of exploration, by touching, pulling, banging, mouthing, or throwing, indicates his level of maturity. In some cases, excessive tactile exploration may represent impulsiveness. A more systematic approach may indicate his need to reinforce visual impressions by tactile and kinesthetic or haptic input.

ASSESSOR'S ROLE AS TEACHER

If the child lacks the ability to organize and sequence tasks, the assessor should provide structure and order. By task analysis it is possible to determine the steps involved, and these can be chained, one to the other, backward or forward, as an adaptation of Skinner's Law of Chaining (1938). Sequencing, which contributes to task accomplishment, can be taught. For example, *chaining* is an effective technique for teaching the mentally retarded. By way of illustration, consider the task of shoe lacing. In the beginning an assessor may perform all but the last step of the process, which is then taught to the child. When the child has completed the step successfully a number of times, the previous step is added until by this backward chaining the child can perform all steps of the task in sequence. The same process can be set up for forward chaining, by having the child perform the first step while the assessor does the remaining ones. Gradually, subsequent steps are added until the child completes the task independently.

An assessor may need to provide input through multiple sensory modalities. He can give directions verbally, which provides auditory input, and he can demonstrate the task, which gives visual input. Touch and movement are other ways of teaching and learning. This multisensory approach stimulates and develops associative processes. Through practice, associations become automatic and promote efficiency. In the field of education a multisensory technique was utilized as early as 1920 by Grace Fernald and among educators is known as simultaneous VAKT (Gearheart, 1976).

Imagery can also be stimulated by helping the child verbalize the task plan, either by questions or by simply requesting that he describe what he is going to do. Imagery is basic to mental manipulation and abstraction.

SUMMARY
Some ideas about learning

There are many different kinds of learning as well as various theories about how learning occurs. Repetition, reinforcement, and *interference* (a term used for factors that increase the likelihood for forgetting) appear to be fundamental elements affecting learning, which, as suggested by evidence from studies, occurs in many places within the brain at once (Dethier and Stellar, 1970). Some authorities believe that memory, the basic necessity, is the result of a structural change in the central nervous system. Experiments cited in the literature (Dethier and Stellar, 1970; Hilgard and Bower, 1975) point to the possible importance of ribonucleic acid (RNA) and protein synthesis in the formation and maintenance of memory. Opinions vary, but Hilgard and Bower believe that conflicting empirical results reduce the plausibility of RNAs role, and Dethier and Stellar indicate that it is by no means clear if effects are due to encoding of memory rather than simply to increased neural activity. As noted, it is currently accepted that memory is spread throughout the cerebrum, and some believe that storage probably exists at all levels of the nervous system, including the spinal cord (Moore, 1973). Injury to specific areas reduces the capacity to remember but does not necessarily destroy specific memories. Experiments and observations support the theory that memory formation is probably a multistage process, different stages being mediated by physiological, biochemical, and anatomical changes and requiring anywhere from a few seconds to a matter of days (Dethier and Stellar, 1970). Short-term memory represents the lowest level and lasts no more than a few seconds. Included among the short-lived impressions are hundreds of sensory messages that are promptly forgotten. Other information may be retained for a few minutes to a few hours, such as a telephone number or a speech. Long-term memory represents preserved information—that which has importance for the individual, is useful, or is associated with a vivid event. It is information that has been sifted out from all the impressions entering the brain. Long-term memory takes time to register permanently on the brain. One hypothesis cites the phenomena of "reverberating" neural activity, stimulated by a particular experience, which continues to persist for a period of time. Supposedly, it is while this reverberatory activity lasts that the permanent structural change, underlying the long-term memory, is slowly developing. When the reverberatory traces die out, the structural change stops and remains at the level attained (Hilgard and Bower, 1975).

Some researchers believe that the limbic system plays a key role in memory. As we have learned, the limbic system is concerned with emotions, drives, and visceral functions. One part of the limbic system, the hippocampus, has been identified as specifically affecting memory function. An individual whose hippocampi, from both hemispheres, have been destroyed or partially removed cannot recall new information for any great length of time, but he continues to maintain long-standing as well as immediate and short-term memory.

Lesions to other areas of the brain give an indication of an area's functional contribution and may result in agnosias or the inability to recognize an object through the senses; aphasia, a form of agnosia resulting in the inability to express oneself and/or comprehend speech; and apraxia, the inability to motor plan. However, it should be understood that these are not discrete entities but differ with the individual and are dependent on personality, chronological age, and the extent and location of the lesion. Since it is unlikely that two lesions of exactly the same size and position will occur, there is bound to be variation from one individual to another.

A speech and language diagnostician specializes in identifying specific language deficits and can obtain information about the child's learning style. This specialist represents another valuable resource person for the assessor of activities of daily living. As an expert in language, the diagnostician can recommend ways for facilitating the communication process between the child and others in the environment.

With injury to the visual association area in the occipital lobe, the individual is unable to recognize common objects visually, although he may be able to do so through using other senses such as touch. This would be considered a visual agnosia. If the injury is in the area of the parietal lobe, he loses his ability to identify an object by touch as well.

An individual may have difficulty in expressing thoughts, although he understands what is said to him. He has an expressive aphasia that may result from a disturbance to the motor speech area (Broca's area) in the left frontal lobe. He may know what he wants to say but cannot say it.

The reverse condition may exist. An individual may not understand what is said to him, which constitutes a receptive aphasia resulting from a disturbance of the hearing association area located in the temporal lobe.

Apraxia has been discussed previously as the inability to motor plan. In other words there is a failure to appreciate the action; one cannot organize a plan to accomplish the motor act. *Kinetic apraxia* is the descriptive term for the inability to carry out purposive movements, which occurs without loss of motor power, sensation, or coordination. A deficit may affect communication. When an individual cannot make a verbal response or gives an incorrect response that is recognized by him as being incorrect, he may have a speech apraxia for words. His motor system as such is not impaired, but rather, he cannot use the motor system effectively to express language. If he is unable to express himself in written form as well, he is said to have *dysgraphia*, a form of apraxia.

Injury to the frontal lobe results in a loss of the ability to deal with the abstract. A child may be unable to make-believe or, at a more complex level, to reason. His responses tend to be concrete.

An additional consideration is the matter of hemispheric specialization. In right-handed people the left hemisphere is dominant, containing areas associated with speech and hearing and, in addition, appearing to be involved with analytical tasks such as solving mathematical problems. The right hemisphere, on the other hand, seems to be more specialized for spatial reasoning and for handling nonverbal perception, including inflection and body language. It is also believed to be more active in the synthesis of ideas and, because of its spatial perceptive qualities, influences the esthetic appreciation of art and music.

Some learning principles

Finally, various authorities, some who specialize in learning theories, propose principles to facilitate the learning process. Ideas come from various schools of thought: from stimulus-response theorists, Gestalt theorists, cognitive theorists, and those who specialize in areas of motivation, personality, and social psychology. Since principles become more meaningful through experience and application, it is more advantageous for an assessor to search the literature directly, thereby forming an immediate acquaintance with a variety of concepts. Since each child is a unique being, principles should be utilized selectively. If an approach to learning is ineffective, it should be reevaluated, perhaps discontinued for that individual, so that optimally only those principles serving to augment the child's performance are employed.

The following generalizations seem relevant to the discussion in this handbook:

- Knowledge is derived from action. Learning comes through the child's own activity.
- Information must be organized, either by the child or through external assistance.
- Frequency of repetition is important in acquiring skill.
- Feedback enables a learner to alter and improve his skill.
- Desirable responses should be recognized.
- Goal setting by the learner provides motivation.
- The kinds of encouragement needed depend on the learner's anxiety level.
- Teaching should match the child's level of development.
- The child learns (adapts to) an independent way of functioning by progressive stages.

REFERENCES

Banus, B. S. 1971. The developmental therapist. Thorofare, N.J., Charles B. Slack, Inc.

Battin, R. R., and Haug, C. O. 1970. Speech and language delay—a home training program. Springfield, Ill., Charles C Thomas, Publisher.

Beadle, K. 1976. A lecture on language and speech disorders (unpublished). Palo Alto, Calif., Children's Hospital at Stanford.

Chaney, C. M., and Kephart, N. C. 1968. Motoric aids to perceptual training. Columbus, Charles E. Merrill Publishing Co.

Dethier, V. G., and Stellar, E. 1970. Animal behavior, ed. 3. Englewood Cliffs, N.J., Prentice-Hall, Inc.

Frostig, M., and Maslow, P. 1970. Movement education: theory and practice. Chicago, Follett Publishing Co.

Gearheart, B. R. 1976. Teaching the learning disabled, a combined task-process approach. St. Louis, The C. V. Mosby Co.

Hilgard, E. R., and Bower, G. H. 1975. Theories of learning, ed. 4. Englewood Cliffs, N.J., Prentice-Hall, Inc.

Luria, A. R. 1960. The role of speech in the regulation of normal and abnormal behavior, Bethesda, Md., U.S. Department of Health, Education and Welfare, Russian Scientific Translation Program.

Moore, J. C. 1973. Sensorimotor integration—a workshop. San Diego, University of California Extension.

Pulaski, M. 1971. Understanding Piaget—an introduction to children's cognitive development. New York, Harper & Row, Publishers.

Sattler, J. M. 1974. Assessment of children's intelligence. Philadelphia, W. B. Saunders Co.

Skinner, B. F. 1938. The behavior of organisms. New York, Appleton-Century-Crofts.

Taylor, E. M. 1971. Psychological appraisal of children with cerebral defects. Cambridge, Mass., Harvard University Press.

9 *Movement and independence*

Movement and independence are linked together, each contributing to the other. Any consideration of independence would be incomplete without including its most measurable modifiers, the mechanical forces that assist or hinder the child as he carries out complicated feats of balance and movement.

"Human motion is a part of all motion, behaving in accordance with the same principles, subject to the same laws as motion occurring in any body, animate or inanimate."* Writing in 1971, Wells further explains: "The basic mechanical principles are derived chiefly from Newton's three laws of motion and from the principles of leverage . . . the specific behavior of the body in its obedience to these principles may vary according to the environment in which it is moving and to the nature of its support."†

We now have some idea of how a child becomes an erect individual, and we know that various sensory modalities aid him in this accomplishment. From a structural standpoint one can marvel at his progression from a quadruped bound to a supporting surface, gradually emerging through stages to an elongated figure extending upward into gravity's field, normally having only two contacts with the earth's surface. To be independent motorically it is necessary to achieve such strength, flexibility, state of balance, and control of body structure through physiological processes or adaptively through the use of external aids.

A TOTALLY EQUIPPED STRUCTURE

The body is a unique architectural structure that has the capacity to change with age. Growth is the most rapid before birth and during the first year of life. The body is engineered for flexibility so that individuals can move easily, freely, and in most instances, without conscious effort. A totally equipped structure, it is made up of millions of cells of protoplasm that group themselves into tissues. Tissues have characteristic qualities and form the organs of the body. Organs perform work for the systems that conduct essential life processes. Although each system

---

*From Wells, K. F. 1950. Kinesiology—the mechanical and anatomical fundamentals of human motion illustrated, p. 26. Philadelphia, W. B. Saunders Co.
†From Wells, K. F. 1971. Kinesiology—the scientific basis of human motion, ed. 5, p. 109. Philadelphia, W. B. Saunders Co.

functions separately, the state of being of one system affects the others. Metabolism and growth, respiration, transportation of materials, nutrition, excretion, reproduction, response to stimuli, and locomotion are conditionally tied together. They are interdependent life systems that adjust, assist, and interact with one another. Movement must be viewed in such a context as a part of a total, continuously adapting structure that houses the individual and serves his being.

TYPES OF BODY TISSUE

The characteristic qualities of the tissues that are the building materials for the body affect its movement. If elastic fibers are bound down, movement is restricted. If the rigid framework, bone, becomes brittle, forces may jeopardize its integrity and movement will be compromised. Tissues, in addition to being hard or elastic, have qualities suiting their functional roles, described as soft, firm, sticky, or tough. Constituting mass, they determine body contour.

Tissues that cover surfaces, line cavities, and form glands are protective and extensible. They make up epithelial tissue found in the external skin surfaces; in structures such as blood vessels, stomach, and intestines; or in the salivary and other glands.

Muscle tissue is made up of three types of fibers: smooth fibers, striated fibers covered by sheaths, or striated cardiac muscle fibers without sheaths joined in a continuous network; all muscle tissues have the common characteristic of contractility. They expand and contract, whether vitally as in the pumping movement of heart tissue or in peristalsis of the alimentary canal, or occur selectively and voluntarily, as when an individual performs a deliberate motor act.

Nervous tissue has previously been examined in some depth. It provides a signaling system and conducts sensory and motor impulses. Specialized characteristics include irritability, conduction, and integration.

Connective tissue supports body structures, from fragile nerves and blood vessels to muscles and organs. It acts as packing tissue, holding structures in place, absorbing pressure, and protecting vital contours. It bandages other tissues, separating them or reducing friction of movement between them, or at strategic points it furnishes a cushion between tissue masses. To provide a total body tensional network, connective tissue has a variable consistency. It may be semisolid such as the reticular framework for the spleen, lymph nodes, bone marrow, or in the opposite extreme it may consist of a solid, rigid matrix of extracellular material found in bone. In between these degrees of hardness and plasticity, connective tissue exists as a strong, pliable tissue forming ligaments, joint capsules, or heart valves. In a solid elastic state it makes up cartilaginous tissue around joints and between vertebrae, capable of absorbing shock and submitting to movement.

Tissues are bathed in water and rightfully so, since interstitial fluid is vital for cell life, carrying in it gases, liquids, and solids. Chemical reactions necessary for body functions occur more readily in a watery solution.

Finally, body tissues are protected by an external covering, the "integument," or skin, which acts as the body's boundary and as an organ of reception for the nervous system. It shields the body against invasion of bacteria, against injury to the more sensitive tissues within the body, against rays of the sun, and against loss of moisture. It is richly supplied with small blood vessels and receives one third of all the blood circulating throughout the body. Being extensible, it yields to tissue bulges and stretches.

MUSCULOSKELETAL SYSTEM

Muscles and bones act together to provide movement. "Without muscles a skeleton would be immobile; and without bones, muscles are merely flesh."[*] Motile body postures are influenced by the nervous system and other factors: by the line of action of muscles as they pull on the bone levers; the joint or joints over which the muscles pass; the relative length of the muscles; the distance of muscles to the axis of motion of a joint; the contours of joint surfaces; the structural balance of the body segments; and the shifting centers of gravity (Brunnstrom, 1962). Efficiency of movement depends on movement conservation. If more muscles are used than are needed, there is extraneous movement and effort.

The skeleton—the body's framework

In embryo most of the "bones-to-be" are cartilage, but after birth, calcium compounds are gradually deposited in the infant's bones, and this process continues throughout life. In children, bones are relatively pliable because they contain a larger proportion of cartilage and a smaller amount of firm calcium salts. With maturation this ratio changes, as does the number of bones. Some of the separate bones in the body become fused so that eventually, as an adult, the number is reduced from approximately 270 to 206 bones.

Bones act as girders for the total body structure, "spacers," if you will, between the ends of muscles. They also provide constant protection from exterior intrusion for the heart, brain, and certain other organs. The rib cage, skull, spinal column, and pelvis encircle vital organs as a shielding suit of bony armor. The long bones making up the extremities give a maximum amount of strength for supporting the body with a minimum amount of material. The flexible stack of vertebrae in the spinal column serves as a pillar of bone to support the head and trunk of the body. At birth the entire presacral vertebral column is extremely flexible, but at 3 or 4 months of age, when the infant begins to hold up his head, the anterior convexity of the cervical portion appears. With upright posture the forward lumbar convexity develops but is not far advanced at 3 years of age (Watson and Lowrey, 1967). These vertebral curves are closely associated with balance and posture. Because they are subject to the slightest stimulation, they are not fully under voluntary

---

[*]From Lyon, D. 1976. Structural integration—a question of balance. San Jose, Calif., San Jose State University (unpublished thesis).

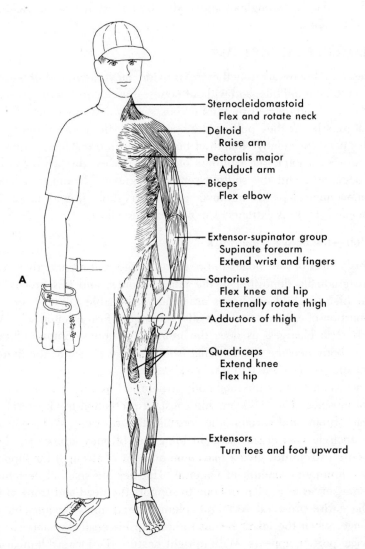

Sternocleidomastoid
  Flex and rotate neck
Deltoid
  Raise arm
Pectoralis major
  Adduct arm
Biceps
  Flex elbow

Extensor-supinator group
  Supinate forearm
  Extend wrist and fingers
Sartorius
  Flex knee and hip
  Externally rotate thigh
Adductors of thigh

Quadriceps
  Extend knee
  Flex hip

Extensors
  Turn toes and foot upward

A

Fig. 9-1. Skeletal muscles, anterior, **A** and posterior, **B**, views. (Drawings by Florence Fujimoto.)

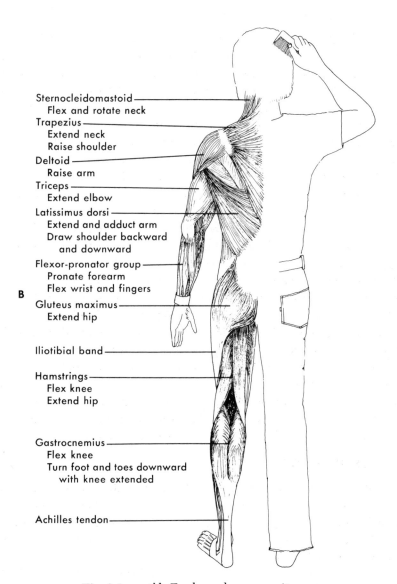

Sternocleidomastoid
 Flex and rotate neck
Trapezius
 Extend neck
 Raise shoulder
Deltoid
 Raise arm
Triceps
 Extend elbow
Latissimus dorsi
 Extend and adduct arm
 Draw shoulder backward
  and downward
Flexor-pronator group
 Pronate forearm
 Flex wrist and fingers
Gluteus maximus
 Extend hip

Iliotibial band

Hamstrings
 Flex knee
 Extend hip

Gastrocnemius
 Flex knee
 Turn foot and toes downward
  with knee extended

Achilles tendon

B

Fig. 9-1, cont'd. For legend see opposite page.

control (Watson and Lowrey, 1967). As was discussed earlier, balance and reaching activity are not mastered until approximately 6 years of age.

At the periphery of the body curved surfaces of bones in the hands and feet permit angular motion and prehension in varying degree.

Muscles—the body's motors

Each muscle fiber is about the size of a human hair, many of which, held together by connective tissue, make up a single muscle. The entire muscle is then encased in a tough connective tissue sheath. There are over 600 muscles scattered over the body, 400 of which are skeletal muscles. Skeletal muscles are of various shapes and sizes, each designed for the job it performs. Some are spindle shaped, wide at the center and tapered at the ends; some spread out from a center line in a fan shape. Muscles may be penniform or featherlike, rhomboidal or rectangular. Most muscles have two or more attachments to the skeleton, and the method of attachment varies. In some instances the connective tissue within the muscle ties directly to the periosteum (covering) of the bone. In other muscles the sheaths and partitions within the muscle all extend to form a cord (tendon), a sheet (aponeurosis), or fascia (membrane) to attach the muscle to the bone. The two ends of an individual muscle are attached to different bones so that when the muscle contracts, one or the other of the bones must move. A large number of skeletal muscles are arranged in pairs. When a muscle (agonist) or set of muscles contracts, there is an opposing muscle (antagonist) or set of muscles that yields to the movement. This antagonist muscle is prepared, on signal, to shift roles and become the agonist, contracting and pulling the bone back in the opposite direction. The agonist-antagonist interreaction is a finely tuned, coordinated action. Other muscles steady the bone, giving "origin" to the prime mover so that only the "insertion" will move, and more muscles steady the joint so that movement is more efficient. When contracting, opposing forces are equal, a state of "cocontraction" exists, and there is increased stability. Strong muscular work requires cocontraction, whereas speed requires less force and more rapid, alternating movement.

FACTORS OF STABILITY

A basic skill for a child performing activities of daily living is the ability to maintain balance under varying circumstances—to shift his position suddenly, to maintain a postural stance, to adjust trunk station without using the arms as accessory props, and to reach out from his midline to the farthest perimeters of his body structure. Balance is related to factors of stability.

The center of gravity varies with body build and shifts if the arms are raised or if a weight is carried above the waist. It then shifts higher and becomes more difficult to maintain. In essence, the line of gravity fluctuates with every change in position. Lowering the center of gravity, along with widening the base, will increase the stability of the body, as in kneeling. A requisite for stability is keeping the center of gravity over the base of support. Additionally, the nearer the line of gravity is to the center of the base of support the greater will be the stability. For example, as the child sits on the floor, he is more secure in maintaining his position when his legs are spread apart. His balance decreases with angular movement as he leans forward, to the side, or backward and decreases still further if he reaches out with his arms. His most stable posture is a vertical line. On the other hand, if an external force is applied, inclining the body and widening the base of support in the direction of the oncoming force increases stability. This generally occurs automatically as an equilibrium reaction to enable him to keep the center of gravity over the base of support in spite of an external force.

The body with its numerous movable parts is a series of structural segments, one placed on top of the other. This increases the demands of the equilibrium task. Maximum stability of a segmented body is assured when the centers of gravity of the segments lie in a vertical line, centered over the base of support. In the body structure, when one segment gets out of line, there is usually a compensatory disalignment of another segment to maintain a balanced position of the body as a whole. This is most strikingly apparent in conditions of asymmetry such as occur in scoliosis of the spine. Segments automatically adjust themselves to maintain a balanced position and, in doing so, usually produce a secondary curve.

IMPLICATIONS FOR ACTIVITIES OF DAILY LIVING

Balance, cocontraction, muscle strength, range of motion, synergy, and postural control are indispensable elements for movement or static position required in self-care tasks. Prognosticating information relating to functional potential can be obtained through muscle testing and range-of-motion examination. This has been presented in the literature as applicable to spinal cord injury by Wilson, McKenzie, and Barber (1974). Predictability is more obscure in the neuromotor problems found in cerebral palsy. Some "key movements," ones that provide prerequisite posture for a task or represent a necessary first sequence of movement to perform independently, will be considered here. These will be identified through looking at developmental sequences in rolling, coming to sitting, sitting, reaching, and grasping. An assessor's ability to make discriminatory observations of neuromuscular and musculoskeletal dysfunction may be sharpened by an awareness of characteristic problems relating to function. Examples include abnormal postures, limitations in range of motion, and weakness and/or disturbed innervation.

Analysis of problems
Voluntary rolling

Voluntary rolling requires the child to turn his head to the side in the direction toward which he is to roll. The key movement, however, is shoulder flexion-adduction, activated by the prime mover, the greater pectoral muscle. Wells (1971) describes this tissue mass as a large, fan-shaped muscle that spreads across the chest, originating along the medial two thirds of the clavicle, the anterior surface of the sternum, the cartilages of the first six ribs, and a slip from the aponeurosis of the external oblique abdominal muscle. It converges toward the armpit, tapering to a flat tendon, which twists on itself in such a way that fibers from the lower origin terminate higher than those originating superiorly. The tendon, 2 or 3 inches in width, inserts along the lateral surface of the humerus, just below the head. That portion emanating from the clavicular area lies close to the anterior deltoid muscle and works with it in the flexion, inward rotation, and horizontal flexion-adduction of the humerus, which brings the arm across the body in the direction of the roll. The movement prepares and begins segmental rotation or movement around the body axis, which allows the child to roll to the side or change from a supine to prone position. The range of motion for shoulder horizontal adduction lies between 0 and 130 degrees. To facilitate an effective roll, the distal end of the humerus should approach the midline. Rotation through the trunk involves the oblique abdominal muscles, but in their absence an individual may utilize adaptive techniques such as pulling on the sides of the bed to roll over.

Examples of problems presented by abnormal postures. Karel and Berta Bobath's contributions in the literature have clarified how primitive reflex patterns interfere with the attainment of function. The examples in this discussion draw from their descriptions.*

TONIC LABYRINTHINE REFLEX

Description. This reflex causes a dominant extensor pattern throughout the body in a supine position. When present, the child lies on his back with his head pushing down against the supporting surface. His shoulders are pulled back with his arms abducted and flexed at the elbows. The legs are inwardly rotated and adducted.

Functional result. Because of his static position, the child cannot bring his arms forward. If he turns his head to the side and tries to turn, retraction of the shoulder prevents his initiating the first part of the segmental roll.

ASYMMETRICAL TONIC NECK REFLEX

Description. This reflex causes asymmetry and shoulder retraction. Its presence can be seen more clearly by active movement of the child's head than by passive rotation. When mild, it is present only when the child tries to do something difficult or is excited. It is usually stronger on the right side.

Functional result. When the reflex is activated, the skull limb is fixed in shoulder retraction and external rotation. Thus the child cannot flex and adduct his arm across his body toward the midline.

Examples of problems presented by restricted range

Description. Restricted range is more frequently the result of two factors: contracture of skin, muscle, or connective tissue and restriction created by changes in the joint surfaces themselves. To turn the head to one side, independently of trunk

*From Bobath, K., and Bobath, B. 1972. Diagnosis and assessment of cerebral palsy. In Pearson, P. H., and Williams, C. E., editors: Physical therapy services in the developmental disabilities, pp. 31-185. Springfield, Ill., Charles C Thomas, Publisher.

movement, requires rotation of the head on the body. This articulation occurs between the cervical vertebrae. The atlantoaxial joint between the first and second cervical vertebrae possesses a unique structure and is considered to be a perfect example of a "pivot" joint. At other cervical joints intervertebral disks, having a compression quality, allow small movement of vertebrae in all directions.

A prime mover in rotation of the head is the sternocleidomastoid muscle, which has two sites of origin, one at the top of the sternum and the other on the medial one third of the clavicle. Running upward, it inserts behind the ear at the mastoid process of the temporal bone and by a thin aponeurosis to the adjacent portion of the occipital bone.

Functional result. Limitations in rotation of the head result from fusion of cervical vertebrae or shortening and tension of the sternocleidomastoid and other musculature contributing stability and movement about the neck. Contractures that inhibit excursion of the arm across the chest involve opposing muscles, including tension of the shoulder extensor muscles (Daniels and Worthingham, 1972).

Examples of problems presented by weakness and/or disturbed innervation. Since muscles are innervated at specific locations along the spinal column, an interruption affects all muscles below the site of disturbance. However, some muscles may be innervated at several adjacent levels and thus, if only partially innervated, may appear weak. Even among individuals injured at identical levels, variations in functional capacity exist because of differences in the amount of spasm present or because of diversity in age, coordination skill, or personal motivation for independence.

Description. With the child lying supine, flexion of the shoulder against gravity is required to bring the arm into position for horizontal adduction. By definition this means that the prime movers, the deltoid and pectoral, must have a minimal grade of "fair" muscle strength. In movement with gravity eliminated less strength is required and a "poor" grade permits motion for positioning purposes. Complete denervation represents the additional loss of sensation that ordinarily remains intact in muscle weakness caused by pain or disuse atrophy. If a disruption of the cord is incomplete, various sensory modalities may continue to function but may be impaired. The sternocleidomastoid muscle has a high innervation by the spinal accessory, or eleventh cranial, nerve at the level of the second and third cervical vertebrae. When intact, this muscle enables the individual to stabilize and rotate his head. The deltoid muscle is innervated lower at the fifth and sixth cervical vertebrae by the axillary nerve, and the pectoral major muscle is innervated by the medial and lateral anterior thoracic nerves at the levels of the fifth through eighth cervical and first thoracic vertebrae.

Functional result. Injury at the level of the fourth cervical vertebra results in a loss of innervation of musculature required for rolling to the side, but turning the head remains intact. Functional potential for rolling to the side is more likely with innervation at the level of the sixth cervical vertebra.

Coming to sitting position

A basic requirement in coming to a sitting position is the ability to raise the head from a supporting surface and to maintain a flexed position against gravity through a partial arc of excursion toward the upright position. As was discussed earlier, the sternocleidomastoid muscle is the prime mover. Flexion of the thoracic and lumbar spine, symmetrically, is facilitated by a long flat band of muscle fibers, the rectus abdominal, which extends longitudinally from the pubis to the lower part of the chest, inserting in the cartilages of the fifth, sixth, and seventh ribs. Initially, motion takes place primarily in the thoracic spine. At the point where the scapulae are raised from the supporting surface, the abdominal muscles become fixators, and the trunk is carried through the remainder of the range by reverse action of hip flexors (Daniels and Worthingham, 1972).

Examples of problems presented by abnormal postures

TONIC LABYRINTHINE REFLEX

Description. Because of extensor hypertonicity, the child cannot flex and raise his head from the supporting surface and cannot move his arms forward.

Functional result. Extensor tonicity increases in the supine position, making flexor patterns difficult to obtain. The side-lying posture decreases tonicity.

SYMMETRICAL TONIC NECK REFLEX

Description. As the child raises his head and lifts his arms forward and upward, there is increased extensor tone.

Functional result. The child falls backward.

SPASTIC DIPLEGIA

Description. There is involvement in all four limbs as well as trunk and neck, but the legs are more involved, resulting in increased extensor tone in the legs.

Functional result. There is a resistance in hip flexion as the child comes to the sitting position.

Examples of problems presented by restricted range

Description. Factors limiting motion in neck flexion include apposition of the lower lips of the vertebral bodies anteriorly with surfaces of subadjacent vertebrae, compression of intervertebral fibrocartilages in front (Daniels and Worthingham, 1972), or cervical fusion. Tension of the upper trapezius and longitudinal ligaments, as well as those which are interspinal and supraspinal, limits bringing the head forward. Tension of the back extensors inhibits flexion between the vertebral bodies. Tightness in the low back from hamstring contracture restricts hip flexion.

Functional result. Limitations in neck or thoracic flexion may require the child to roll to his side and push himself to the sitting position through elbow extension and shoulder depression. Tightness in the hamstrings, two joint muscles originating on the ischial tuberosity and inserting below the knee, may cause the legs to flex when the child comes to a sitting position or require him to put his legs over the side of the bed, thereby putting the hamstrings on slack through knee flexion.

Examples of problems presented by weakness and/or disturbed innervation

Description. The role of the sternocleidomastoid muscle in raising the head from the supporting surface has already been considered. An analysis of trunk flexion indicates that it is the strong longitudinal rectus abdominal muscle, innervated by the lower intercostal nerves at the seventh through twelfth thoracic vertebrae which provides symmetrical flexion. A muscle grade of "good" is required for an individual to come to a sitting position without using the arms as accessory props, and fixation is given both by the reverse action of the hip flexor muscles and the weight of the legs and pelvis.

Functional result. Loss of innervation of the abdominal muscles does not prohibit independence in coming to a sitting position through adaptive techniques and equipment. Even a lack of grasp in holding on to a bed trapeze can be compensated for by using straps looped about the forearms. Strong elbow flexion by the biceps and brachioradial muscles is a necessity. Although these are partially innervated at the fifth cervical vertebra, the absence of other prime movers about the shoulder (the latissimus dorsi, pectoral, serratus anterior) and the incomplete innervation of the stabilizers prevent the remaining musculature from becoming functional. Innervation at the sixth cervical vertebra contributes partial, but significant, musculature about the shoulder, and most importantly, the appearance of radial wrist extensors provides a source of substitute grasping for holding on to suspended trapeze loops. Thus, even with the absence of conventional grasp, the individual can adaptively use equipment and mobilize his strength in elbow flexion to sit up independently or to assist in the task. With innervation at the seventh cervical vertebra, the individual is virtually assured of gaining independence in coming to a sitting position and may even be able to approach complete wheelchair independence. The addition of the triceps muscle enables him to stabilize his elbow in extension, and this, in turn, permits him to utilize fully innervated shoulder depressors in lifting his body weight from the supporting surface—a feat that has significance for bed mobility and transfer skill.

Sitting

Maintaining an erect sitting posture requires first and foremost the orientation of the head in space and postural control of this body segment. Brunnstrom (1962) points out that a minimum of effort is exerted by the extensor muscles in keeping the head erect, since its center of gravity is only slightly anterior to the transverse axis of the atlantooccipital joint. However, since the head is frequently moving, particularly during activities, this effortless alignment is often interrupted. Nonetheless, fatigue is uncommon, unless the forward position of the head is maintained over a long period. In addition to the upper trapezius, numerous short muscles situated deeply under the skull assist in neck extension.

Trunk stability or the balance of the vertebral column depends largely on the posterior trunk muscles. The entire extensor group is known as the erector spinae, or sacrospinalis, muscle, which consists of two parallel, longitudinal branches with each branch having many separate slips. It originates as a large mass in the lumbosacral area and soon divides into its two branches. Tendons emerge along the way, inserting into the transverse processes of the vertebrae and angles of the ribs. The uppermost strand of muscle extends lateralward and upward to insert to the mastoid process of the temporal bone.

Support of the spine, particularly under conditions of strain, is also provided by anterior trunk musculature, the abdominals and intercostals. The abdominal wall consists of four abdominal muscles, their fibers encased in sheaths arranged in layers that run in different directions. This has the effect of strengthening the wall and supporting the abdominal viscera. The rectus abdominal muscle is superficial, running longitudinally on either side of the linea alba, a fibrous band in the midline of the abdomen. This band unites the aponeurosis of the muscles of the right and left sides. The oblique external abdominal is also superficial and is lateral to the rectus, its fibers running obliquely and aiding in trunk flexion, along with rotation. The oblique internal abdominal lies below and the transverse abdominal composes the innermost layer of the abdominal wall. The intercostal muscles located between the ribs functionally are a continuation of the external and internal oblique abdominal muscles.

When supporting trunk musculature is weak or absent, the child will need protective extension of his arms to maintain erect posture and, additionally, support to his back as in propped sitting. Broadening his base of support through positioning his legs away from the midline will extend lines for the center of gravity. If necessary, the center of gravity can be lowered, as in reclining the back of a wheelchair that is providing propped support.

Examples of problems presented by abnormal postures

ASYMMETRICAL TONIC NECK REFLEX

Description. When the child turns his head to the side, his arms automatically assume a fencing position and extension of the face limb and external rotation, retraction, and flexion in the skull limb.

Functional result. The child is limited in protective extension of his arms to one extremity, since the skull limb is flexed. He may compensate by attempting to keep the head down to avoid the asymmetrical tonic neck reflex, which is strongest in extension, or to avoid sudden startle reactions, which upset his balance when he is trying to look up.

SYMMETRICAL TONIC NECK REFLEX

Description. This reflex causes a dominant flexion or extension pattern of the arms and an opposite posture pattern in the lower extremities, depending on the position of the head. When the child lowers his head, there is an increase in flexor hypertonicity of the upper extremities and he slumps forward. Sitting posture is made more difficult by a narrow sitting base caused by adductor hypertonicity of the legs and increased extensor tone, resulting in lack of balance.

Functional result. By adaptation the child may achieve a sitting posture. Both types of hypertonicity are then present, and the total flexion or extension pattern cannot be seen. He learns to compensate through kyphotic posture, which may become permanent. In time he may develop flexion contractures of the hips and knees.

SPASTIC DIPLEGIA

Description. There is increased muscle tone in the lower extremities with massive flexor or extensor patterns. The whole body may be involved but to a lesser extent than the lower extremities.

Functional result. The child's sitting base is more stable as he brings his head and spine forward. Flexion of the hips enables him to abduct the thighs and flex his knees. The pelvis is tilted forward and the spine is stiff.

SPASTIC QUADRIPLEGIA

Description. The whole body is affected, but the upper extremities are equally or more involved than the lower extremities. There may be increased extensor spasticity caused by stimulation of touch and pressure receptors of the buttocks as they come in contact with supporting surfaces.

Functional result. Difficulty in sitting is increased because of the inability or difficulty in flexing the thighs at the hip joints.

Examples of problems presented by restricted range

Description. Tension of the hamstring muscles prevents the child from flexing his hips to 90 degrees. Two-joint muscles passing over the hip and knee include the semitendinous, semimembranous, and biceps femoris muscles.

Functional result. Insufficient hip flexion in a sitting position results in compensation through the spine whereby the child brings his head forward over the sitting base. In time this results in kyphosis.

Examples of problems presented by weakness and/or disturbed innervation

Description and functional result. Although a child with interruption of innervation at the first thoracic vertebra level still lacks trunk stability and trunk fixation for the upper extremity prime movers, he has full innervation of the upper extremity musculature, allowing good protective extension of the arms. Trunk stability increases with innervation at the sixth thoracic vertebra through the long muscles of the upper back and the upper intercostals. At the twelfth thoracic vertebra, innervation of the rectus abdominal, the obliques, the transverse abdominal, and all muscles of the thorax provides a fully stable trunk. Weakness exists primarily in the low back, where lumbar musculature is not innervated. Potentially, the child with innervation at the twelfth thoracic vertebra is a candidate for full independence in all self-care activities, including wheelchair and ambulation with aids.

Reaching and grasp

As the arms extend outward from the body, the center of gravity rises and balance is less stable. Movement of the arms necessitates the child making quick shifts in position to maintain balance. If the arms must perform heavy work, cocontraction is required at the proximal joints and at the midline to stabilize and maximize the force exerted by moving muscles.

To reach all body parts, including those at the periphery, the child must actively move his scapulae and shoulders in all planes available to him through flexion, extension, internal and external rotation, adduction, and abduction. Flexion and extension at the elbow calibrate reaching parameters toward his head or feet for essential activities of daily living. Finally, combinations of range at the shoulder, elbow, and wrist bring the hand, with its valuable prehensile qualities, in contact with body surfaces superiorly. Flexibility of the spine and range at the hips and knees permit the child to reach all the way to his toes.

Grasping involves complex movements. Long muscles pass over several joints, thus potentially affecting movement in multiple locations. An example is the tenodesis action of the long wrist extensors and flexors that affect excursion of the fingers in grasping. Wrist extension is necessary to place extensors on slack so that full finger flexion for grasping can be obtained. "The most powerful wrist action, whether hyperextension or flexion, can take place only when the fingers are relaxed. Strong finger action requires a rigid wrist, and a strong wrist action requires relaxed fingers."* The functional position of the wrist is considered to be 30 degrees of dorsiflexion and 0 degrees to slight ulnar deviation.

Other positions necessary for effective prehension include rotation and abduction of the thumb for opposition to the finger volar pads. Similarly, slight flexion of the fingers at the metacarpal, phalangeal, proximal interphalangeal, and distal interphalangeal joints is needed to position the fingertips for prehension. Some authorities consider 45 degrees of flexion at the proximal interphalangeal joints as optimum. Varying degrees between pronation and supination place the hand in angular planes for carrying out manual skills, such as in writing, feeding, bathing, shaving, applying deodorant, and cleansing after a bowel movement.

Examples of problems presented by abnormal postures

ASYMMETRICAL TONIC NECK REFLEX

Description. The child's arms assume a fencing posture when he turns his head to one side.

Functional result. The child may adaptively use the asymmetrical tonic neck reflex for reaching. Generally his grasp is weak, and he releases objects too easily unless he also has a tonic grasp, which makes it difficult for him to extend his fingers for prehension and, similarly, to open his hand for release. The asymmetrical tonic neck reflex inhibits the child's visual search; it prevents his looking at an object as he grasps it. His eyes may be fixed toward the side to which the face is turned, and he cannot follow objects beyond the midline. Furthermore, he cannot bring his fingers to the mouth because he can only bend his elbow when he turns his head away from the arm. The reflex is usually stronger on the right side so that children with this abnormal reflex use the left hand dominantly. Eventually, the child may develop scoliosis along with subluxation of the hip joint of the skull leg.

SPASTIC DIPLEGIA

Description. There is a lack of stability around the hip because of a narrow sitting base.

---

*From Wells, K. F., and Luttgens, K. 1976. Kinesiology; the scientific basis of human motion, ed. 6, p. 129. Philadelphia, W. B. Saunders Co.

Functional result. The child can use only one arm and hand for grasp, since the other must be used for stabilizing the sitting posture. If he reaches out with both arms, he tends to fall backward. He makes excessive compensatory movement of the head, upper trunk, and arms in utilizing available righting reactions present above the waist.

SYMMETRICAL TONIC NECK REFLEX

Description. The reflex produces flexor tone in the upper extremities and extensor tone in the lower extremities when the head is lowered.

Functional result. The child may utilize this abnormal reflex to hold with his arms and grasp with his hands. However, he cannot use his arms to reach out from his body. The hips and legs tend to extend and adduct.

Examples of problems presented by restricted range

Description. Whenever there is a restricted range about a joint, compensation becomes necessary at other joints. With multiple joint involvement, as in arthritis, compensation becomes self-limiting.

Functional result. When body surfaces cannot be reached by the hands, adaptive equipment may be utilized to provide the extension or flexion required. To use equipment effectively, the child may need a firm grasp and stabilization in the midline, coupled with patience and a tolerance for equipment.

Examples of problems presented by weakness and/or disturbed innervation

Description. Reaching and grasping require active movement of the arms against gravity, combined with neck and trunk stability and cocontraction at joints proximal to moving joints. Innervation of musculature has been reviewed. To summarize, decisive muscle groups are innervated predominantly at the following levels: (1) the deltoid muscles of the shoulder and the biceps muscle of the shoulder and elbow are innervated at the fifth cervical vertebra; (2) the pectoral major which adducts the arm across the chest, the latissimus dorsi which extends the arm, the serratus anterior which abducts and rotates the scapula upward, and the radial wrist extensors are innervated at the sixth cervical vertebra; (3) the triceps which extends the elbow, along with long finger extensors and flexors, are innervated at the seventh cervical vertebra; and (4) the intrinsic muscles lying within the hand which permit fine, precision movement as in opposing the thumb to volar pads of the fingers are innervated at the first thoracic vertebra. As indicated previously, innervation of some muscles may occur above or below the levels given here.

Peripheral nerve injuries affecting muscles of the hand result in characteristic deformity and loss of function. A median nerve injury is described as an "ape hand" with the thumb in the plane of the hand. There is an inability to oppose or flex the thumb, and sensory losses may be demonstrated over the distal phalanges of the middle and index fingers and thumb. A radial nerve injury results in a "drop wrist." There is extensor paralysis with sensory disturbance on the dorsal radial surface of the hand. Grasping ability is decreased, since the extensors are on stretch. An ulnar nerve injury presents a "claw hand" appearance with hyperextension at the metacarpal phalangeal joints of the ring and little fingers. There is an inability to spread

EQUIPMENT LIST																	

Key: 0 . . . Does not need
      + . . . Has equipment item
      R . . . Needs—recommend purchase

Visit number	1	2	3	4	5	6	7	8	Visit number	1	2	3	4	5	6	7	8
BED AIDS									TOILETING AIDS								
Hospital bed									Bars								
Side rails									Raised toilet seat								
Foot board									Commode								
Trapeze									Cleansing aid								
Sheepskin									Adapted panties								
Sandbags									Incontinence pants								
Prismatic glasses																	
									FEEDING AIDS								
DRESSING AIDS									Swivel spoon								
Dressing stick									Rocker knife								
Sock aid									Suction base								
Reachers									Plate guard								
Button hook									Utensil holder								
Adapted fastenings									Straw holder								
									Feeding splints								
									Slings								
HYGIENE AIDS									Ballbearing feeders								
Sponge																	
Hand brush																	
Hair brush cuff									TRANSFER AIDS								
Skin inspection mirror									Sliding board								
Electric toothbrush									Hoyer lift								
Adapted towel									Bathtub lift								
									Bathtub bars								

EQUIPMENT

the fingers or to oppose all the fingertips and thumb as in making a cone. Sensory loss is evident on the ulnar side of the hand, specifically over the entire little finger.

Functional result. Orthoses and adapted equipment may permit the child to increase his level of independence in the presence of muscle weakness or loss of innervation. This has been well documented by Wilson, McKenzie, and Barber (1974). Special aids include mobile arm supports, flexor hinge splints which may be electrically powered, motorized wheelchairs, seating inserts, electric typewriters, and a variety of aids for feeding, dressing, hygiene, and transfer activities. Examples are provided on the accompanying equipment list.

EQUIPMENT LIST—cont'd																	

Key: 0 . . . Does not need
    + . . . Has equipment item
    R . . . Needs-recommend purchase

Visit number	1	2	3	4	5	6	7	8	Visit number	1	2	3	4	5	6	7	8
TRANSFER AIDS—cont'd									**STANDING and/or AMBULATION—cont'd**								
Bathtub bench									Crutches								
Gutter loop									Tilt board								
									Standing table								
									Flexie prone cart								
WHEELCHAIR									Ramp								
Standard									Helmet								
Semi-reclining									Guerney								
Full-reclining																	
Elevating legrests																	
Swinging footrests									**COMMUNICATION AIDS**								
Desk arms									Pencil holder								
Removable arms									Paper/holder								
Seat belt									Typing sticks								
Cushion									Electric typewriter								
Brake extensions									Telephone dialing aid								
Desk top									Tape recorder								
Crutch holder																	
Electric (motorized)																	
Motorette attachment																	
STANDING and/or AMBULATION																	
Corset																	
Braces																	
Surgical boots																	

REFLECTION

With the conclusion of this chapter a realistic inventory of an assessor's skills becomes broader and increasingly identifiable. Assessment of a child's self-care ability requires an understanding of the neuromotor development that occurs in infancy and precedes the child's capacity for voluntary function. It includes an awareness of the coping mechanisms that occur, with influences from family, peers, community, and culture on the adaptation process. A foundation in neuroanatomy and neurophysiology contributes to an analysis of perception's role in the performance of self-care tasks, and task analysis helps an assessor to observe how the child learns. With this fund of information an assessor must still be able to explain function on the basis of the most visible evidence, the motor performance.

REFERENCES

Bobath, K., and Bobath, B. 1972. Cerebral palsy. I. Diagnosis and assessment of cerebral palsy. In Pearson, P. H., and Williams, C. E., editors: Physical therapy services in the developmental disabilities. Springfield, Ill., Charles C Thomas, Publisher.

Brunnstrom, S. 1962. Clinical kinesiology. Philadelphia, F. A. Davis Co.

Daniels, L., and Worthingham, C. 1972. Muscle testing, techniques of manual examination, ed. 3. Philadelphia, W. B. Saunders Co.

Lyon, D. 1976. Structural integration—a question of balance. San Jose, Calif., San Jose State University (unpublished thesis).

Watson, E. H., and Lowrey, G. H. 1967. Growth and development of children, ed. 5. Chicago, Year Book Medical Publishers, Inc.

Wells, K. F. 1950. Kinesiology—the mechanical and anatomical fundamentals of human motion illustrated. Philadelphia, W. B. Saunders Co.

Wells, K. F. 1971. Kinesiology—the scientific basis of human motion, ed. 5. Philadelphia, W. B. Saunders Co.

Wilson, D. J., McKenzie, M., and Barber, L. 1974. Spinal cord injury—a treatment guide for occupational therapists. Thorofare, N.J., Charles B. Slack, Inc.

10 *Administering the activities of daily living assessment*

It has been established that an activities of daily living assessment is structured so that an assessor may gather specific data on identifiable behavior. In reality an assessor must view these specific behaviors within the context of the total environment and total responses present. Background information interweaves the technical data being assembled. Therefore an assessor's professional skill includes more than recording specific responses; it requires processing global observations. The significance of these observations is strengthened by the assessor's ability to classify them into areas of function, that is, physical, social, emotional, perceptual motor, or intellectual.

ASSESSOR'S INFLUENCE ON THE ASSESSMENT PROCESS

Concomitantly, an assessor must consider his own impact on the child. Awareness should extend from the external environment to within himself; it is necessary that he reach a state of perceptiveness which enables him to measure the influence of his actions and attitudes on the child and, later, on others who share in the assessment process. This awareness permits him to use himself, through interaction, as a tool to facilitate maximal performance of the child. In addition, an assessor should be able to identify options open at any given moment and mentally forecast the consequences that may result from a choice of action. Alertness in all these areas permits the assessor to maintain control and to exercise flexibility in managing the assessment process.

An example of an assessor's perceptiveness is the accuracy with which he detects and interprets verbal and nonverbal communication of the child and parent. Factors such as voice tone, facial expression, and body posture give messages. Verbal content can be analyzed not only in terms of what is said but also by shifts in conversation, pauses, the association of ideas, and recurrent references (Garrett, 1942). The relationship between assessor and client depends, in part, on the assessor's understanding of the urgency of the messages given.

The assessor must be able to understand the emotions present in those who cope with disability. As the child and parent present themselves, there must be a willingness to hear whatever is said and to respond by utilizing professional and technical skills while conveying concern. Listening alertly and with interest does not mean agreement with what is being said. It means, at the appropriate time, giving clarity to the confusion that may result from a lack of knowledge and a sense of helplessness.

THREE PHASES OF ASSESSMENT

There are three phases to consider in carrying out an assessment: pre-assessment preparation; creating an environment that elicits the most accurate and maximal performance; and bringing to conclusion the technical and professional aspects of assessment.

Phase 1. Preassessment preparation
Gathering information

Prior to meeting the parent and child there is information to be gathered and arrangements to be made. To prepare materials needed during the assessment and to be knowledgeable of medical and psychological precautions, the assessor should read available records, noting age, diagnosis, significant history, and restrictions.

Organization

Good assessment technique requires organization, and this begins immediately through selecting a means of depositing information that will be needed in writing up the assessment results. One method is to establish a working folder where notes, orders, and assessment forms may be collected. Depending on the setting and book-keeping system, it may be prudent to check financial coverage and note which agencies are involved.

Scheduling the appointment

In scheduling the appointment, the assessor should consider a number of factors. Of utmost importance is the child's age, attention span, usual daily routine, and fatigue level. The assessor must also be aware of other scheduled appointments and evaluate their demands on the child's physical and emotional energy. Once the appointment is selected and the location determined, the assessor or a reliable clerical assistant notifies and confirms the time with the parent and child. To assure that essential information has been given, the individual making the contact checks to determine that the parent knows how to reach the assessment area or, if indicated, clarifies how contact will be made. It is important to communicate any change in plans and convey this to the parent, child, and other affected persons as soon as possible.

Location and materials

A location, free from distractions and interruptions, permits the assessment to proceed more efficiently and smoothly. The assessor will be in a position to devote full attention to the performance if he has carefully thought through the steps of the assessment and the materials required. These may include clothing articles, food appropriate for the child, utensils, and adaptive equipment. The child's age and predictable behavior may require that toys be available to relieve anxiety, to provide purposeful distraction, as time-out relaxation, or as a reward system.

Phase 2. Creating an environment that elicits the most accurate and maximal performance
Introductions

Initial contact with the parent and child constitutes the beginning of the next phase, which is creating a climate that elicits the most accurate and maximal performance. The assessor begins by introducing himself to all members present, clarifying names carefully and with interest. Should there be an observer, a student or colleague, he or she is also introduced and permission to be present during the assessment is requested. The child's or parent's right to exclude an observer must be acknowledged attitudinally as well as formally.

Explaining the purpose of the assessment. The usual approach for discussing the assessment is to explain its purpose; for example, "An activities of daily living assessment identifies strengths and deficits in performing self-care tasks. It enables the assessor to make a plan for helping the child learn skills leading to independence." An explanation must also be given to the child, at a level he can understand, and should contain specifics of just what the assessor will do and what he will ask the child to do.

The assessor may note anxiety on the part of the child through facial expression, clinging to the parent, or lowering his head. Such reactions may be associated with what the child perceives as an intrusion into his most personal functions by a stranger with whom he has little or no relationship. The assessor should acknowledge the child's right to privacy and take the time to work through his feelings about the assessment and its personal aspects. A combination of dignity, composure, warmth, respect, and understanding characterizes a professional approach, and the assessor's demeanor assists the child in gaining ease in what can be an uncomfortable situation.

Parental concerns. Once the purpose of the assessment is discussed, there should be an exploration of parental concerns. Specific topics can be introduced: expectations for the assessment, what parents see as problems to be solved, and what long-range consequences they anticipate from current problems. Parents are sometimes understandably concerned over distant goals—whether their child will be able to go to college, live alone, marry, have children, and be a wage earner. They may seek reassurance that their goals are achievable. The child as an adult can be a paramount concern, even though the activities of daily living assessment focuses on the here and now. Unless an assessor responds to parental concerns in his report, the parent is left coping with unanswered questions and unrelieved anxieties, feeling inadequately equipped to set realistic expectations. Knowing the parents' priorities, regardless of whether answers can be produced through the activities of daily living assessment or some other evaluation, gives a clue as to how feedback should be given and in what order. This does not change "findings" but only the manner in which they are presented.

In concluding the initial contact, the parent should be told when the assessor will respond to the points raised, that is, after the assessment data are gathered and studied, after consultation with other staff members, and after presentation to the physician in charge of the case.

Observations of the performance

Having responded to the parent, the assessor can now focus attention on the child and his performance. Factors influencing normal motor behavior have been outlined in Chapter 5. Chapters 6 to 9 discuss other aspects that influence the child's performance. Subtle responses, including exploratory behavior, can be important in making interpretations as to the causes of his difficulties and in making recommendations for treatment. Responses and conditions can be organized according to function.

Physical function. Is posture symmetrical? Are there abnormal postures? What is the pattern of prevailing posture? Are there associated reactions? What is the quality of muscle tone—type, degree, changes? Can the child change positions? What is the quality and speed of movement? Of equilibrium?

Is there weakness? Are there contractures, deformities, or atrophy? Are joints enlarged or swollen? Are there pressure areas on the skin? Is endurance appropriate?

Do the eyes focus together? What is the quality of eye movements? Are pursuits carried out vertically and horizontally? Is there evidence of visual ignoring on the right or left side?

Social function. Does he initiate conversation? Is there eye contact? Does he like to be touched or does he pull back? Does he regard others in his surroundings?

Emotional function. What is the child's frustration tolerance? If a child is reluctant to perform, is it because of a fear of failure, a resistance to exposing real or imagined inadequacies? How does he cope with stress? What is his energy level? Does he ignore parts of his body? Does he display facial animation? What is his body posture?

Perceptual motor function. Is it necessary to demonstrate the task or even passively take the child through the task such as in putting an arm through the sleeve of a shirt? Does he sequence the task appropriately? Does he know front from back? Does he understand concepts of "up," "down," "in," and "out"? Can he identify right and left sides of his body? Does he avoid crossing the midline? Are bilateral movements skillfully executed? What is his hand dominance? Is he easily distracted? By what? Is he impulsive? Do his eyes follow his hands at work? Does he locate articles near him? Does he disregard certain extremities?

Intellectual function. How does the child approach a task—impulsively, trial and error, analytically, or automatically? How does he problem solve? How does he respond to verbal directions? How many steps of a task can he process at one time? Does he remember sequences? Is his thinking concrete or abstract? Does he show safety judgment?

Process-oriented relationship

It has been further established that an activities of daily living assessment is not a standardized test. The assessor is free to involve himself, indeed is obligated to do so, because a part of the assessment is to discover what factors enhance the child's performance. It may be motoric, placing the child in postures that break up mass flexor or extensor patterns. Responses may be altered by the application of sensory stimulation, whether tactile as in brushing or tapping, proprioceptive as in joint approximation, or vestibular as in rocking. It may also be a matter of organizing stimuli and breaking the tasks down into steps that the child can comprehend—and of giving reassuring support.

Throughout the performance the assessor should be alert to clues, carefully noting signs of mental or physical fatigue such as changes in posture, flushing, rubbing eyes, stifled responses, or crying. These may be signals for time-out or that the assessment should be carried over to another day. In concluding the session, the assessor acknowledges the child's efforts, cites tasks that are examples of his best performance, and indicates what kind of help he may expect with problem areas. The child, unlike the parent, requires immediate feedback.

Phase 3. Bringing to conclusion the technical and professional aspects of assessment

Compiling the results—scoring and analysis

Again an orderly progression with tasks enables the assessor to synthesize the material. The scoring of each item on the assessment form should be checked. Comparisons among items should be considered. Are particular tasks similar in their requirements, for example, demanding more complex perceptual motor skill such as required in "fastenings"? In what areas does the child perform most strongly and why? Where are the weak areas and causes? What motivates the child? How does he direct his energy? How does his performance measure up to parental expectations? What cultural and socioeconomic factors are of significance? What are realistic short-term and long-term goals?

Scoring the activities of daily living assessment. A scoring system is often the most controversial feature of an assessment form. This may be partly because, as therapists refine data, they are sometimes likely to overextend analysis, with the result that the scoring system becomes complicated and readily understandable only to the individual preparing the report. Establishing criteria for the symbols of measurement helps to limit such expansion.

Three factors are set forth for the model presented in this handbook: The symbols for scoring must have clarity; there can be no more than five symbols so that the visual memory is not overstressed; and the symbols have to be acceptable to a computer.

SYMBOLS. Since a computer best utilizes numerical units, numbers from 0 to 4 are set down in a graduated scale of levels of independence.

4 . . . Independent
3 . . . Independent with equipment and/or adaptive technique
2 . . . Completes independently but not in a practical time
1 . . . Attempts but requires assistance or supervision to complete
0 . . . Dependent, cannot attempt
— . . . Nonapplicable

A more complete definition of each level of independence is necessary to enable the assessor to make decisions as to the appropriate symbol to use.

4 . . . Independent. This symbol means the capacity to carry out a task alone, without help, within a practical time limit with required endurance. Patterns of movement should be smooth, primitive reflexes should be integrated, and muscle tone should be normal.

3 . . . Independent with equipment and/or adaptive technique. This symbol means the capacity to carry out a task alone, without the help of an assistant but with equipment aids if necessary, within a practical time limit. Patterns of movement may be uncoordinated; primitive reflexes may be evident or present residually through increased muscle tone; associated reactions, that is, released postural reactions that may produce a widespread increase of spasticity in all parts of the body, may be shown. Postures may be exaggerated to lend stability. The task may be carried out in a compensatory way, that is, through an adaptive technique.

In marking the assessment, the assessor grades independent performance having any of these characteristics as a grade 3. In the recommendations attached to the assessment, he gives observations on reflex activity, asymmetry, associated reactions, contractures, deformities, and weaknesses. He states whether the technique used by the child is acceptable or whether it should be altered and how. If he considers that the activity is inappropriate for the present, he recommends a treatment plan to prepare the child for the task. If gaps are present, he points out skills to be developed. It is generally agreed that therapists interrupt and normalize patterns of movement in infancy through early childhood when the nervous system is more plastic, whereas with adolescence, emphasis shifts to "function" and abnormal reflexes may in fact be utilized to achieve more function.

2 . . . Completes independently but cannot accomplish in a practical time. "Practical time" can be challenged as a variable factor depending on an individual assessor's judgment. The reality, however, is that attempting to set standards becomes exceedingly complicated with a rapidly changing organism, the child. Philosophically, there is merit to the belief that practical time needs to be determined on an individual basis, if this is possible, with consideration being given to factors such as demands in the home, the daily time schedule, and even the structure of the home. Parental and patient attitudes may also be determining elements in time requirements. If not in a testing situation, they may still surface to affect performance on a day-to-day basis. The influence, however, may be subtle and unclear.

1 . . . Attempts but requires assistance or supervision to complete. This would signal the physician that some attendant care is required.

0 . . . Dependent, cannot attempt. Full attendant care is needed.

— . . . Nonapplicable. This may indicate that the activity is developmentally inappropriate. Medical restriction, as in a case of hip dislocation or postspinal fusion, may prohibit motor activity required by the item.

Finally, if a child refuses to do a task, a note should be made and considered in determining the validity of the assessment.

• • •

The details of scoring, analyzing data, organizing findings, and presenting recommendations may be best assimilated at this point through a case presentation. Utilizing the portion of the assessment pertinent to feeding activities, the observations of a therapist are given as he assesses a child who is 2 years 9 months of age with the diagnosis of spastic quadriplegia as a result of anoxia at birth from aspiration pneumonia.

In *propped sitting*, defined as the ability to sit with the trunk erect, head and chin lifted, and with back supported, the assessor observes that the child's head is not maintained in midline and drops forward. Both the child's head and trunk drift to the left. The child makes attempts to right his head, but frequent repositioning by the mother is required. The assessor notes that the child fails to use the arms in a propping reaction and gives the performance a grade 1—attempts but requires assistance to complete.

In *sitting, hands props*, defined as sitting alone passively without support, with hands acting as an accessory prop, the assessor again notes that the child is unable to adjust to changes in posture of his head and lacks propping reactions. The performance is given grade 0—dependent, cannot attempt.

In *sitting unsupported*, defined as sitting unsupported indefinitely, with hands and arms freed for manipulatory duty, and eyes elevated, a grade 0 is given.

In *reaching to midline*, defined as the ability to bring the hands together at the center of the body and grasp an object with a two-handed approach from a supine position, the assessor notes that the child's hands engage only momentarily at midline. A grade 1—attempts—is given for right and left hands.

In *reaching to mouth and face*, defined as the ability to grasp and bring an object to the mouth or face in a sitting position, the assessor observes that the child's grasp appears reflexive and immature with excessive force. He does get his hands to his face alternately. Grade 1 is given for right and left hands.

In assessing *swallow*, defined as the ability to gather up food and squeeze it to the back wall of the throat, thereby stimulating a swallowing reflex, the assessor observes that the child shows mild tongue thrust. There is evidence of a sucking reflex and imperfect approximation of the lips. Nonetheless, the child swallows without requiring external stimulation and the assessor gives a grade 3, indicating independence with the presence of abnormal patterns.

In *suck and use a straw*, the assessor again notes poor sealing of the lips, mild tongue thrust, and immature sucking. Little liquid is obtained by the child and a grade 1 is given.

In *chew* (semisolids, solids), defined as the ability to masticate solids by well-defined chewing, the assessor notes overbite and sees only vertical movements with no rotatory chewing and gives a grade 1.

In *finger foods*, defined as the ability to reach, grasp, and bring finger food to the mouth, the assessor again notes the child's crude grasping ability. Only occasionally does he manage to acquire a piece of cracker. He does get his hands to his mouth, however. A grade 1 is given for right and left hands.

Under *utensils*, defined as the ability to grasp utensils, fill or filled with food and raise them to the mouth without spilling, the assessor watches the child swipe at the utensil, but he cannot open and prehend it. If a utensil is placed in his hand, he cannot maintain his grasp on it. This performance receives a grade 0.

In preparing an interpretation of the data, the assessor utilizes observations and organizes them under findings and recommendations as follows:

Findings

1. There is inadequate head and trunk control for function.
2. Increased extensor tone in the face limbs is demonstrated when the head is turned to the side (tested by feeling muscle tone in the child's limbs as the head is moved from side to side).
3. Little or no propping reaction of the arms is evident.
4. The child demonstrates a reflexive type of grasp with little or no voluntary release. Hands engage only momentarily in the midline.
5. Sucking reflex is present with mild tongue thrust. There are vertical chewing movements only with no rotatory chewing. The child demonstrates overbite and sensitivity about the mouth with imperfect approximation of the lips.

Recommendations

1. Study the "feeding" history obtained from the parent, noting responses to various foods in terms of texture, consistency, taste, and temperature.
2. Position the child on the prone board to stimulate a propping reaction of the arms and righting reaction of the head.
3. Maintain the child's head in the midline for feeding and keep his chin down.
4. Stimulate the child's use of his lips to pull food from the spoon. Inhibit his tongue thrust by pressing down on the tongue with a soft infant spoon.
5. Use a straw to stimulate sucking (not reflexive type) as a preparation for speech.
6. Delay the use of utensils until the child's hand function further matures. In the meantime attempt to do the following:
   a. Desensitize primitive hand reflexes.
   b. Facilitate hand movements (materials, textures, objects) and encourage eye-hand regard.
   c. Differentiate mass head and arm movements. Manually resist abnormal postures that result from primitive reflexes during head activity. This may

eventually weaken the reflex activity and contribute to differentiation of the head and arm movement as suggested by Mysak, 1968.*

Writing the report. Sattler (1974) describes the written report as the vehicle of communication. Accordingly, it needs to provide an accurate, incisive description of the child and to convey useful, meaningful recommendations. The assessor should present findings clearly, recognizing the readers' interests and concerns. Content should be carefully communicated in terms that the receivers will comprehend. Sattler compares the readers of the report to consumers who may have diversified backgrounds. He believes that efforts should be directed toward writing clear, objective reports with a minimum of technical jargon and a maximum of simplicity. With experience one gains such perspective—to value simplicity and strive for it while appreciating the complexities of the assessment process and its professional nature.

Content of the report

The report focuses on three areas: (1) findings in the form of functional measurement of the performance, (2) areas of strength and deficit, and (3) recommendations. Material may be organized in different ways, but it is advisable for an assessor to develop a consistent format such as that which follows.

Identifying information. Include the name of the facility, title of the assessment, name of the patient, medical chart number, date of birth, chronological age, diagnosis, and date of report.

Reason for referral. Note any problems indicated by the referral source. Indicate concerns voiced by the parents or child. Include pertinent facts from the medical and/or psychosocial history.

General observations. State where the assessment was conducted and, if significant, who was present. Briefly describe the child's physical status, that is, ambulatory or nonambulatory. Note the child's hand dominance. Cite attitudes and feelings and identify any significant evidence of stress created by the assessment. Determine if there is a balance of activity in the child's daily schedule, that is, work, pleasure, or rest.

Findings. Present results categorically according to the activities of daily living form with documentation of the level of function, along with a clarifying explanation of why the child is able or unable to perform independently. Briefly summarize total performance according to the child's strengths and deficits.

Recommendations. Be specific and practical. Try to answer referral questions and concerns of the parents or child. Indicate your level of confidence in the recommen-

---

*Dr. Edward O. Mysak states: "Essentially, this is accomplished by positioning the individual in an appropriate positive symptom inhibiting posture and then passively lateralizing the head, bending the head in an ear-to-shoulder fashion, as well as ventroflexing and dorsiflexing the head. These head movements are carried out while the clinician resists the emergence of tonic reflexes. . . . Other parts of the body should be differentiated following similar maneuvers, the goal being to help the child develop the ability to move an arm, leg, forearm, foot, finger, and so on, in isolation." From Mysak, E. O.: Neuroevolutional approach to cerebral palsy and speech, p. 46. New York, Copyright 1968 by Teachers College, Columbia University.

dations, for example, whether there is potential for increased independence with training or equipment. Determine available services in the community, resources of the family, and the competency of services available.

Signature. Give the assessor's name and title.

The draft

As an assessor gains experience, he will be able to organize and put down information more quickly and clearly. Sattler (1974) advises that the student likely will need to go over his first draft sentence by sentence or word by word. Regardless of skill in writing, careful proofreading will always be necessary.

One technique in report writing is to put aside the draft for a day or so, if possible, and then return to it for reading. In this way the writer may be able to scrutinize the clarity of the material more accurately and recognize errors. Judgment as to whether statements are unclear and vague can be made with greater objectivity after thought processes are allowed to settle and rest, even for a short period of time. The exclusion of inferences, loaded words, drawing a distinction between fact and interpretation, deciding on the advisability of including examples with substantiative statements can be comprehended and judged by the writer more clearly when he can approach his own writing as a potential reader.

Sattler (1974) poses a thoughtful question to the writer of an assessment: "Can the report be understood by an intelligent layman?" If so, the writer has rendered a service to his client, the child, by helping others understand the child's performance.

One last point is that the first impression a report makes on a reader is often directly related to the neatness of its appearance. A cardinal rule is to take the time to correct spelling, grammatical, and typing errors to the best of one's ability.

Presenting the results—the assessor as consultant

Physician. Finally, the results are presented to the physician, then to the parent, and if appropriate, to the child as well. Centers will vary in their philosophy about the best way to give results to parents—whether findings should be presented directly by the different disciplines or whether the information should be sent to the physician, who then interprets the materials as a whole and sets up an overall plan.

Case conference. From my experience the most effective delivery results when staff members involved in the case meet together in a case conference to compare results, validate findings, and combine their recommendations carefully to avoid mixed messages. Such decisions as to whether a parent should be involved in a home treatment program can be determined through the therapist's outline of the intellectual, physical, and emotional demands of the program and the social worker's evaluation of the family's competency in carrying through and its effect on family relationships.

Details concerning how information should be presented to the parents emerge through discussion. The success or failure of this expensive communication system may later depend on the group's sensitivity to what the parent is able and willing to hear and the sense of timing with which information is given. There are choices in the form of presentation, whether oral, written, or both. Often parents have as great a need to hear about what they are doing correctly as to be told about the problems that exist.

Case conferences are more efficient when resources within the child's community have been researched prior to the meeting and financial ability and responsibility have been clarified. Such information is needed to determine the feasibility of recommendations. Responsibility for ongoing care also needs to be clearly defined and the frequency of follow-up determined. When appropriate, plans should be formulated to mobilize the community and to assist agencies through providing pertinent information from the case conference.

Parents and child. Sattler (1974) suggests that the crucial test of the effectiveness of the communication with the parents and child is whether they are able to act on the basis of what they have learned about the assessment results. In some cases several interviews may be needed. Recognizing and adjusting to the realities of a child's limitations involves emotional and intellectual adjustment and can be aided by identifying strengths that exist.

An additional consideration in some cases would be a home visit, which permits the assessor to gain an understanding of the child's and parents' natural environment and the forces exerted within it, be they architectural barriers or some other form of obstacle or strengthening agent. A further understanding of coping skills and individual life-styles may enable professionals to help the family effect change and adaptation if that is indicated.

CONCLUSION

The skills of assessment are not easily acquired. They go beyond the technical level, yet contain requirements for specific tasks as well as abstract principles that enable one to determine the kind of response to make in each situation and when flexibility is warranted in monitoring the assessment process.

Like an art, assessment skill is developed through application, in an evaluation of one's own performance and by an observation of colleagues. Skill is perfected by clinical experience and increased awareness of appropriate factors. Assessment skill contains many elements, but most noteworthy is the delicate analysis of the child's disability, how he copes, and how those important in his life—parents, siblings, peers, and teachers—respond to his efforts.

REFERENCES

Garrett, A. 1942. Interviewing—its principles and methods. New York, Family Service Association of America.

Mysak, E. D. 1968. Neuroevolutional approach to cerebral palsy and speech. New York, Teachers College Press.

Sattler, J. M. 1974. Assessment of children's intelligence. Philadelphia, W. B. Saunders Co.

11 *Supplementary assessment forms*

The seventy-six tasks selected for the basic assessment can only be considered fundamental ones. Some children will need supplementary assessment of wheelchair and transfer skills or written communication. The adolescent brings new tasks to be achieved with his or her physical maturation and additional emerging needs for independence in household tasks, community activities, and vocational skills.

Included in this section are forms covering some of these areas.

addressograph stamp	**CHILDREN'S HOSPITAL AT STANFORD OCCUPATIONAL THERAPY** **TIME-ORIENTED RECORD** **ACTIVITIES OF DAILY LIVING ASSESSMENT**		

Key to scoring: 4 . . . Independent
3 . . . Independent with equipment and/or adaptive technique
2 . . . Completes but cannot accomplish in practical time
1 . . . Attempts but requires assistance or supervision to complete
0 . . . Dependent—cannot attempt activity
— . . . Nonapplicable

	Visit number	1		2		3		4		5		6		7		8	
	Julian date																
	COMMUNICATION	R.	L.	R.	L.	R.	L.	R.	L.	R.	L.	R.	L.	R.	L.	R.	L.
	Writing																
1	Sharpen pencil																
2	Print																
3	Write																
4	Erase																
	Typing																
5	Insert paper																
6	Press space bar																
7	Press key																
8	Turn carriage																
9	Remove paper																
	Telephone																
10	Remove receiver																
11	Hold receiver																
12	Dial																
13	Speak																
14	Replace receiver																
15	Take message																
16	Use telephone book																

ACTIVITIES OF DAILY LIVING

<table>
<tr><td colspan="2" rowspan="2">

addressograph stamp</td><td colspan="17">**CHILDREN'S HOSPITAL AT STANFORD OCCUPATIONAL THERAPY**

TIME-ORIENTED RECORD

ACTIVITIES OF DAILY LIVING ASSESSMENT</td></tr>
</table>

Key to scoring:
- 4 . . . Independent
- 3 . . . Independent with equipment and/or adaptive technique
- 2 . . . Completes but cannot accomplish in practical time
- 1 . . . Attempts but requires assistance or supervision to complete
- 0 . . . Dependent—cannot attempt activity
- — . . . Nonapplicable

Visit number		1		2		3		4		5		6		7		8	
Julian date																	
ADOLESCENT SELF-CARE		R.	L.	R.	L.	R.	L.	R.	L.	R.	L.	R.	L.	R.	L.	R.	L.
	UNDRESSING																
1	Remove nylons/panty hose																
2	Remove girdle/garter belt																
3	Remove brassiere																
4	Remove necktie																
	DRESSING																
5	Put on nylons/panty hose																
6	Put on girdle/garter belt																
7	Put on brassiere																
8	Put on necktie																
	AIDS																
9	Put on eyeglasses																
10	Remove eyeglasses																
11	Put on hearing aid																
12	Remove hearing aid																
	HYGIENE																
13	Shampoo hair																
14	Set hair																
15	Shave face																
16	Shave underarms																
17	Shave legs																
18	Apply deodorant																
19	Apply makeup																
20	Groom fingernails																
21	Groom toenails																

ACTIVITIES OF DAILY LIVING

		CHILDREN'S HOSPITAL AT STANFORD
		OCCUPATIONAL THERAPY
		TIME-ORIENTED RECORD
addressograph stamp		**ACTIVITIES OF DAILY LIVING ASSESSMENT**

Key to scoring: 4 . . . Independent
3 . . . Independent with equipment and/or adaptive technique
2 . . . Completes but cannot accomplish in practical time
1 . . . Attempts but requires assistance or supervision to complete
0 . . . Dependent—cannot attempt activity
— . . . Nonapplicable

	Visit number	1	2	3	4	5	6	7	8
	Julian date								
	TRANSFERS								
	Specify: ambulatory								
	with crutches								
	with wheelchair								
1	To bed								
2	From bed								
3	To toilet								
4	From toilet								
5	To bathtub								
6	From bathtub								
7	To shower								
8	From shower								
9	To regular chair								
10	From regular chair								
11	To car								
12	From car								
13	To bus								
14	From bus								

ACTIVITIES OF DAILY LIVING

		CHILDREN'S HOSPITAL AT STANFORD OCCUPATIONAL THERAPY TIME-ORIENTED RECORD ACTIVITIES OF DAILY LIVING ASSESSMENT
addressograph stamp		

Key to scoring: 4 . . . Independent
3 . . . Independent with equipment and/or adaptive technique
2 . . . Completes but cannot accomplish in practical time
1 . . . Attempts but requires assistance or supervision to complete
0 . . . Dependent—cannot attempt activity
— . . . Nonapplicable

Visit number		1		2		3		4		5		6		7		8	
Julian date																	
WHEELCHAIR SKILLS		R.	L.	R.	L.	R.	L.	R.	L.	R.	L.	R.	L.	R.	L.	R.	L.
1	Sitting balance																
2	Fasten belt																
3	Unfasten belt																
4	Lock brakes																
5	Unlock brakes																
6	Propel forward																
7	Propel backward																
8	Propel corners																
9	Open doors																
10	Close doors																
11	Go up ramp																
12	Go down ramp																
13	Raise footrests																
14	Lower footrests																
15	Swing footrests to side																
16	Remove arms																
17	Replace arms																
18	Pick up object from floor																
19	Sitting push-ups (10)																
20	Adjust position																
21	Reach crutches, holder																
22	Place crutches, holder																

ACTIVITIES OF DAILY LIVING

addressograph stamp	**CHILDREN'S HOSPITAL AT STANFORD OCCUPATIONAL THERAPY** **TIME-ORIENTED RECORD** **ACTIVITIES OF DAILY LIVING ASSESSMENT**								

Key to scoring: 4 . . . Independent
3 . . . Independent with equipment and/or adaptive technique
2 . . . Completes but cannot accomplish in practical time
1 . . . Attempts but requires assistance or supervision to complete
0 . . . Dependent—cannot attempt activity
— . . . Nonapplicable

Visit number	1	2	3	4	5	6	7	8
Julian date								
HOUSEHOLD ACTIVITIES								
Food preparation								
1 Open: milk								
2 packaged food								
3 bottles, capped								
4 screw lids								
5 Pour: liquids								
6 dry ingredients								
7 Mix: with spoon								
8 egg beater, manual								
9 electric mixer								
10 Sift flour								
11 Break egg								
12 Peel vegetables/fruit								
13 Cut vegetables/fruit								
14 Use: measuring spoons								
15 cups								
16 can opener								
17 rolling pin								
Range								
18 Operate: burner controls								
19 oven controls								
20 Place pans on range								
21 Remove hot pans from range								

ACTIVITIES OF DAILY LIVING

Continued.

| | | CHILDREN'S HOSPITAL AT STANFORD OCCUPATIONAL THERAPY TIME-ORIENTED RECORD ACTIVITIES OF DAILY LIVING ASSESSMENT |

Key to scoring: 4 . . . Independent
3 . . . Independent with equipment and/or adaptive technique
2 . . . Completes but cannot accomplish in practical time
1 . . . Attempts but requires assistance or supervision to complete
0 . . . Dependent—cannot attempt activity
— . . . Nonapplicable

	Visit number	1	2	3	4	5	6	7	8
	Julian date								
	Range—cont'd								
22	Oven: open								
23	place pans (2-4 lb.)								
24	remove pans (2-4 lb.)								
25	Broiler: in								
26	out								
27	Storage areas: open								
28	close								
	Refrigerator								
29	Open								
30	Close								
31	Food: in								
32	out								
33	Handle ice trays								
	Sink								
34	Dishes, utensils: wash								
35	dry								
36	store								
37	Faucets: reach								
38	turn on/off								
39	Wash sink								

ACTIVITIES OF DAILY LIVING

		CHILDREN'S HOSPITAL AT STANFORD								
		OCCUPATIONAL THERAPY								
		TIME-ORIENTED RECORD								
		ACTIVITIES OF DAILY LIVING ASSESSMENT								

Key to scoring: 4 . . . Independent
3 . . . Independent with equipment and/or adaptive technique
2 . . . Completes but cannot accomplish in practical time
1 . . . Attempts but requires assistance or supervision to complete
0 . . . Dependent—cannot attempt activity
— . . . Nonapplicable

	Visit number	1	2	3	4	5	6	7	8
	Julian date								
	Table								
40	Set								
41	Clear								
42	Serve food								
	Shopping								
43	Make list								
44	Travel to store								
45	Carry parcels								
46	Handle money								
47	Store purchases								
	Cleaning								
48	Use: dust cloth								
49	dust mop								
50	broom								
51	dust pan								
52	Clean: stove								
53	wash bowl								
54	toilet								
55	Empty waste basket								
56	Floors: wash								
57	polish								
58	vacuum								

ACTIVITIES OF DAILY LIVING

Continued.

<table>
<tr><td colspan="3"></td><td colspan="8">

CHILDREN'S HOSPITAL AT STANFORD
OCCUPATIONAL THERAPY

TIME-ORIENTED RECORD

ACTIVITIES OF DAILY LIVING ASSESSMENT

</td></tr>
</table>

Key to scoring: 4 . . . Independent
3 . . . Independent with equipment and/or adaptive technique
2 . . . Completes but cannot accomplish in practical time
1 . . . Attempts but requires assistance or supervision to complete
0 . . . Dependent—cannot attempt activity
— . . . Nonapplicable

	Visit number	1	2	3	4	5	6	7	8
	Julian date								
	Cleaning—cont'd								
59	Furniture: polish								
60	vacuum								
61	Bed: change								
62	make up								
	Laundry								
63	Clothes: wash								
64	hang								
65	dry								
66	fold								
67	Ironing: dampen								
68	set up board								
69	set up iron								
70	put away clothes								
	Sewing								
71	Thread needle								
72	Tie knot								
73	Use straight pins								
74	Use scissors								
75	Sew button								
76	Mend								
77	Use sewing machine								

ACTIVITIES OF DAILY LIVING

		CHILDREN'S HOSPITAL AT STANFORD OCCUPATIONAL THERAPY TIME-ORIENTED RECORD ACTIVITIES OF DAILY LIVING ASSESSMENT

Key to scoring:
4 . . . Independent
3 . . . Independent with equipment and/or adaptive technique
2 . . . Completes but cannot accomplish in practical time
1 . . . Attempts but requires assistance or supervision to complete
0 . . . Dependent—cannot attempt activity
— . . . Nonapplicable

	Visit number	1	2	3	4	5	6	7	8
	Julian date								
	Child care								
78	Bathe								
79	Dress								
80	Undress								
81	Feed								

ACTIVITIES OF DAILY LIVING

12 *Illustrative report*

The illustrative report that follows will demonstrate some, but by no means all, of the principles subscribed to in this handbook.

The assessor compiling the report involves the client in the assessment process and draws out his perceptions of problems and goals. He notes strengths the client displays and determines those factors which interfere with the client's ability to perform independently in activities of daily living. He attempts to view the client's function in relationship to the current demands of life tasks, and he considers the impact of the client's status on the family. He views the client within his community setting.

In his recommendations the assessor indicates his level of confidence in the client's ability to improve his independent-dependent status and introduces specific items (adaptive equipment) for consideration. An interdisciplinary approach is emphasized in follow-up care to further determine abilities and resources so that the client can make long-range decisions—in this case, ones relating to future vocation and, ultimately, living arrangements.

As a case presentation, the report coincidentally illustrates some of the coping required at a turning point in life, from adolescence to adulthood.

CHILDREN'S HOSPITAL AT STANFORD
Activities of Daily Living Assessment Report

Name: JOHN SMITH   Medical Chart No. 49-05-21
Birth date: 5/29/60
Chronological age: 17-2
Medical diagnosis: Cerebral palsy, tension athetoid with underlying spastic quadriplegia
Date of report: 8/10/77

Reasons for referral

John was referred to occupational therapy by Dr. Richard Brown for a comprehensive assessment in activities of daily living. The patient, who has had cerebral palsy from birth, has undergone extensive therapy programs most of his life. He is now completing his high school education. The purpose of seeing him is to review his dependency status, set realistic goals for achieving further independence, and through interdepartmental efforts, assist him and his family with future vocational planning and living arrangements. John's concerns include not only what plans to pursue but where and how to obtain the help he needs, both in career guidance and with sources of financial assistance.

General observations

John has been seen individually in a therapy room for seven evaluation periods and once in his home setting between July 29 and August 8, 1977. He is essentially a severe athetoid, ambulatory by motorized wheelchair, and able to perform assistive standing-pivot transfers. Speech is impaired, but thought processes are good. He is pleasant and personable.

John showed interest in the assessment, volunteered information, and indicated his priorities for assistance. He appears to have an accurate understanding of his limitations and some recognition of the adaptations necessary to cope. Areas of self-care that are most important to him in trying to be more independent are personal hygiene, including toileting. His motorized chair has been an important source of independence in exploring space in his neighborhood, but there are both architectural and transit barriers to mobility in the community at large.

Assessment findings

John will continue to require assistance in most areas of self-care for the rest of his life. A description of his performance is as follows:

Bed. In a supine position, fluctuating asymmetry of extremities is shown with efforts to speak. Increased muscle tone can be felt in both upper extremities when the head is turned to the side, more on the right than the left (positive asymmetrical tonic neck reflex).

In rolling to his side, flexion of his lower extremities aids in flexion of his arms, which facilitates rolling over (mass patterns).

John cannot initiate sitting up. Once his legs are placed over the bed and a flexion pattern is begun, he can pull, holding to an attendant's arms, and come to a sitting position without head lag. He uses fisted hands as props in sitting, and his head control is steady with periodic neck extension. John's muscle tone may fluctuate on movement with hypertonicity to hypotonicity, and his movements are jerky and unpredictable, lacking midranges.

In reaching activities, John shows sustained attention with his eyes. He must exert obvious effort and concentration to control movements of his arms and hands. Digits are extended in reaching, and a unilateral approach with forearm pronated is common. Associated reactions, with facial grimacing and increased athetoid movements, are seen with efforts to move. He can alternately bring his hands to the midline, to his mouth and face, above his head, and behind his head. Although he is able to put his hands in position to work, with elbows and wrists flexed, he then has great difficulty in opening his hands to prehend and, similarly, difficulty in opening them to release. Bilateral use of his hands is an added problem. He has difficulty in bringing the right hand to the midline simultaneously with the left hand (asymmetrical tonic neck reflex). His control of isolated finger movements is poor but better in his right hand. However, he uses his left hand dominantly, which may be related to the stronger asymmetrical tonic neck reflex activity on the right side.

Thus, with maximum effort, John has achieved some measure of control in his neck and eye movements and in trunk stability and balance. He adapts and makes use of the asymmetrical tonic neck reflex for reaching and, additionally, has some voluntary control of movement at his shoulder and elbow and in extrinsic hand musculature for gross grasp. He lacks the control necessary for fine manipulation. He cannot achieve or maintain wrist position and movement, release and grasp, forearm supination, and individual finger manipulation required for fine motor function.

Feeding. John shows little or no drooling; he swallows well, and the tongue rises slightly but there is no thrust. A slight overbite is present, but he manages liquids and solids and seals his lips satisfactorily. Chewing is appropriate, but rotatory movements are reduced. His jaw, on occasion, deviates to the right, which may result from the asymmetrical tonic neck reflex influence.

With effort John can manager finger foods, but the use of utensils is a laborious task and the plate-to-mouth pattern is erratic. Prehension is slow and inaccurate. A cup and glass are even more difficult to grasp than utensils, and his inability to execute a smooth release results in spilling.

Toileting. John controls his bladder for extended periods, up to 6 hours, but sometimes has "accidents," and the area of toileting is high on his list of priorities for achieving independence. He requires an athletic supporter for comfort. Pants' fastenings are a problem, not only because of poor hand skills but also because of getting both hands to the midline simultaneously. John sits on the toilet for bowel movements, and at home it is equipped with a bidet that he can operate. Toilet bars give him security when sitting. He requires assistance in a standing-pivot transfer to and from his wheelchair.

Hygiene. John's bathroom at home has been modified. However, he needs to be able to swing his footrests to the side to work at the sink. He must flex his knees to 90 degrees or beyond to achieve sufficient hip flexion to lean over the sink. He can turn the special faucets on and off and wash and dry his hands and face. To prepare his electric toothbrush, he needs a flat surface directly in front of him.

He is assisted to a shower chair for bathing and pushed to a modified shower, with a portably mounted head, that is situated off the hallway. John is hesitant to lean forward in the chair to reach the controls.

Dressing. John can put a pull-down garment over his head and pull it down, but he cannot button it. He can unbutton but cannot push a shirt over his shoulders. Dressing the lower extremities is even more difficult. Attendant care is required for most aspects of dressing.

Transfers. John can assist with transfers, and by holding on to an attendant's shoulders, he pulls to a standing position, takes several small steps, and sits down. If he becomes caught in an extension pattern, pressure to the stomach and flexion of the neck aids in stimulating a flexion pattern so that he can assume a sitting posture.

Communication. John cannot dial a telephone. Maintaining prehension and holding the telephone to his ear influence the quality of his speech production. The time involved in printing his name is nonfunctional, and his signature is not consistently legible. Typing is exceedingly slow, using the index finger of his right or left hand, and requires excessive energy as well as time.

Entrances to the home. The entrances are ramped, but John cannot operate the doorknobs.

Hobbies. John enjoys a stamp and coin collection and growing plants but is dependent on others to help him pursue these interests. He seeks recommendations.

Summary

John and his family are approaching a crucial, stressful period as he completes his high school education, and they recognize that long-term plans for care must be formulated. To this point the family has made numerous modifications in the home to facilitate John's care. His mother, particularly, appears to have expended sustained effort and energy in developing John's potential—physically, socially, and intellectually. John, in his home setting, seems comfortable with his dependent relationship with his mother, although he can intellectualize a desire to gain more independence. John's parents waiver in their expectations but appear genuinely concerned about his transition to adulthood.

John is basically social, enjoying conversation and group activities. His strengths appear to be his ability to receive, comprehend, synthesize, and organize information; his personal-social skills; his appearance; and his interest in the world about him.

Problems in function result from severe motor impairment, particularly fine hand skills. Motor patterns tend to be massive, and there is fluctuating difficulty in speech production. This combination greatly inhibits his avenues for independent action, including verbal expression. John experiences considerable fatigue at the end of the day.

Recommendations

1. The realities of John's limited physical independence need to be clarified with him and his family. This may require several interviews or may be handled even more effectively

through informal contacts. The emphasis now should be focused on residual function rather than treatment. John will continue to need assistance with personal care, including toileting. It is desirable that this care be shifted to a male attendant as soon as possible, which may help John to accept, more comfortably, the assistance he needs with this personal function and relieve his probable anxiety concerning dependence on his parents, particularly his mother. He should prepare for shifting dependence to persons other than family members with the goal of developing initiative in organizing and directing an attendant in care tasks. Health care teaching in John's program should reinforce his responsibility in providing information to others who assist him.

2. John's potential for improving self-care status appears to be limited, given the degree of involvement, and will depend largely on the utilization of adaptive equipment. Specific suggestions are listed here, along with the recommendation that John be seen on an outpatient basis for 45 minutes weekly for twelve sessions to determine the feasibility of the following equipment aids:

   a. Electric bed with controls—come to sitting position.
   b. Adapted glass, placemat—feeding
   c. Change handle on urinal to accommodate a pronated grasp—toileting
   d. Adjust swinging mechanism for leg rests—to get closer to working surfaces
   e. Make sliding shelf over bathroom sink—flat surface to prepare toothbrush
   f. Provide shower chair strap—for security when washing himself
   g. Velcro fasteners—dressing
   h. Push-button telephone with adjustable arm or speaker phone—communication
   i. Tape recorder—school work
   j. Stamp—signature
   k. Levers, European style—to open doors of home

3. At 17 years of age life tasks include identity in the male role, a realistic appraisal of strengths and weaknesses, preparation for economic independence, emotional independence, and moving out of the home. The process for John will take longer than for most young adults and will require careful planning and preparation, but it should be activated now.

Close coordination between social service, school, and occupational therapy is needed to assist the family and John. Part of this will consist of "information giving," such as eligibility for assistance, appropriate agencies for vocational guidance, other community resources, and alternatives to living at home. Role playing can be used in helping John to gain knowledge and confidence in handling life tasks such as interviewing and selecting applicants for attendant care. Consideration of a peer-counselor should be explored for the purpose of role modeling, and counseling on sexual function should be available on John's request.

John's life would be greatly enriched if more transportation were available in the community so that he could begin to achieve independence in social activities without help from his parents. His ability to relate to others is a major strength and needs to be utilized fully in bringing him satisfaction and a sense of worth and value. He will need to make decisions regarding groups with whom he wants to identify and formulate ideas about his own life-style. Information on groups and their program should be provided, and leisure-time activities should be expanded to capitalize on his social skills.

4. Psychometric testing would be useful in further defining John's intellectual strengths and weaknesses and in determining appropriate areas for vocational direction. Consultation with school personnel is needed so that John can be supported appropriately in setting realistic goals.

5. Case conferences with John and his parents should be held periodically to reevaluate progress toward the recommendations set down and to determine any additional ones.

JANE JONES, OTR
Registered Occupational Therapist

13 Problems that may occur during the assessment— remarks to a new assessor

Various problems may arise to challenge an assessor of an activities of daily living performance, the most common ones coming from three areas: the assessment form, interaction with the child, and response of the parent to evaluation results. Some situations have been described in earlier chapters and surface again for attention. However, this brief discussion is intended primarily as counsel to the new assessor, to reassure the one undertaking the assessor role for the first time that the experienced professional also encounters these problems. Suggested ways of handling problems will be offered for consideration, and philosophical views, admittedly representing my bias, will be provided at opportune intervals.

ASSESSMENT FORM

Perhaps one reason that so many different assessment forms exist is because therapists employ different methods in collecting data or because physicians to whom they give their results have distinct preferences for report content. Different disabilities present different types of problems in self-care and may require specialized lists of task items. Regardless of the reasons, a new therapist in the field will come in contact with many kinds of assessment forms designed to measure level of function. The forms are not standardized, although some items may be based on standardized scores. It is difficult to foresee how levels of independence might be standardized, but a similar query may have existed for those pioneers of psychometric testing at the turn of the century. Certainly, qualities of reliability and validity are appropriate requirements for measurement tools, of which the activities of daily living form is one. For the time being, therapists in the clinical field continue to refine the instrument they use to the best of their ability.

The form in this handbook is one such attempt. Although each activity is defined, the complexity of each individual task makes scoring a gross estimate at best. The details of how an activity is attempted or accomplished by the child may be highly significant, particularly for measuring future progress. Thus, in addition to scoring, details may need to be documented on the lines provided on the back of the form. It is just such a seemingly minor decision that may confront and confuse the new assessor—When should one elaborate on the performance? My inclination is to advise that when in doubt, elaborate. Noting details, particularly as one begins the assessor role, will help a new therapist to build associations between his observations and levels of function attainable by the child and assist with recall skill. With broader experience less description about the performance may be necessary, both for recall and interpretation. I also encourage the new assessor to refer to the definitions for activities when checking the scoring. This may seem time consuming initially, but by following such a pattern, the assessor is more likely to increase the accuracy of his report and sharpen his observation skills.

The user of an activities of daily living assessment form will experience instances when an individual child being assessed presents exceptions and fails to fall within the scoring range, according to the definitions laid down. Health care workers readily acknowledge that each child possesses a physical, social, emotional, and intellectual uniqueness. Yet the assessor is charged to reduce a performance to a list of numerical figures, suitable for a computer, an understandably challenging task, since uniqueness resists classification. When an assessor judges that he cannot score a child's performance on an activity of daily living item, he can give instead a note of explanation.

There may be occasions when the assessor feels dissatisfaction with the form or decides that data may be gathered on the basis of observation alone, without the tedious process of scoring. A point to be made is that when an assessor uses the form to its best advantage, a constructive process of discipline is set in motion. Through its structure the form requires a certain consistency from the assessor. Used from beginning to end, it tends to prevent the assessor from drawing impulsive conclusions. It also reduces his subjectivity, assists him in identifying behaviors, and provides a framework for systematizing the collection and analysis of data.

INTERACTION WITH THE CHILD

There are justifiable reasons why a child would not want to demonstrate his abilities in self-care. The most obvious is the personal nature of the tasks. For most children, activities of daily living are "tasks," and not particularly enjoyable ones. They are daily necessities that can become areas of conflict between the child and his parents, developing into issues involving eating habits, standards of cleanliness, clothing style, and other practices. When attitudinal struggles, feelings of depression, poor self-image, or difficulty in performing are included as well, it becomes more understandable why the child lacks enthusiasm for performing or may even respond negatively. Attitudes may exist at a subconscious level, below the child's level of awareness. Therefore he may be unable to interact verbally, to discuss his reasons for resisting the assessment because he, himself, is not fully cognizant of why he feels the way he does. An assessor may need to spend several sessions preparing the child for the assessment, discussing the reasons for its being done and why cooperation is needed, allowing the child first to demonstrate what he can do before focusing on his deficits or items of a personal nature such as dressing and toileting.

Children feel less threatened when the assessment is depersonalized; for example, the young apprehensive or negative child may be able to interact with a puppet, to express his frustration and anger to this imaginary friend who does not threaten or control him and can speak to his innermost needs or respond understandingly to his expressive, explosive responses. The child may be able to enter into games of self-care tasks when he is not the only loser.

The distractible, hyperactive child challenges both the management skill and energy capacity of the assessor. A fairly obvious first step to take is to remove distracting material from the environment and eliminate unnecessary sounds. Other measures include giving "firm" touch to focus attention as well as verbal input to assist the child in organizing his responses. A reward system may be necessary to provide incentives for following directions and altering impulsiveness.

When working with the adolescent client, negative responses may appear more direct but are not necessarily so. They may represent diversionary tactics for delaying procedures viewed as being unpleasant. Verbal reactions may consist of explicatory statements such as, "That's stupid!" "I can do everything for myself." "I don't need any help. I know what I can do and what I can't do." It is a common reaction for a therapist to feel rejected in instances of verbal retort, even to experience a momentary sense of personal failure. If overcome with a feeling of inadequacy, the assessor fails to respond to and pursue the central problem, that is, why the patient or client feels the way he does. The adolescent may be fearful of exposing his deficits. He may feel clumsy and self-conscious of the struggle he must make to perform. He may feel anger about the circumstances with which he must cope daily or feel resentment at what he perceives as intrusion. Generally, little is to be gained from a power struggle; relations may unexpectedly reach a delicate balance with an adolescent who is striving to erect defenses and maintain control and independence. The adolescent's response may be representative of his defense system, one possibly of denial and avoidance of those situations that increase his emotional discomfort. Adolescents can sometimes be drawn out by strategic questions: "What do you hope to accomplish during this hospitalization?" "Who will help you?" "How long will it take?" "Do you have plans for the future?" "What kinds of things give you satisfaction now?" "What kinds of things have you enjoyed in the past?" "Do you think I can help you?" "May I come back to see you another time?" Skillfully presented questions allow the adolescent to maintain control and to utilize his defenses until stress is alleviated or trust and confidence are established with the assessor. Once such a relationship is firm, the assessor is in a better position to challenge the adolescent and assist him in altering unfavorable coping patterns. In the meantime the content of the adolescent's response may be equally as valuable as a systematized assessment in determining how to mobilize sources for assistance, particularly if the information is channeled to a helpful professional such as a counselor or social worker.

It is discouraging when a child gives a poor performance. On such occasions a new assessor may think he has nothing of significance to report. Attitudes of other professionals may seem to validate this. It is a human trait to be enthusiastic about potential for growth and pessimistic about deficits. Regardless of findings, a goal for a new assessor is to become secure with his ability to assess, and a goal of assessment is the accuracy of its findings. When a child gives a poor performance and potential for change appears limited, there is a constructive focus to maintain. For example, parents may expend energy in a fruitless endeavor, such as pursuing unrealistic treatment goals, when their efforts could be better directed toward attaining small gains in the child's performance. Areas that bring greatest satisfaction to the child may be overlooked in a search for dramatic change. Redirected energy is a valuable outcome of an assessment. In instances where a child is emotionally disturbed or profoundly retarded, an assessor may collect helpful data on performance, noting those things in the environment that elicit particular responses. These observations can be helpful in promoting the child's optimal status and assisting the medical staff to make decisions on recommendations for placement.

RESPONSE OF THE PARENT TO ASSESSMENT RESULTS

Just as an assessor must be sensitive to the responses of the child, so must he be equally perceptive to those of the parent. In this respect the social worker is a valuable counsel to an assessor, both in interpreting parental responses and in facilitating the communication process between assessor and parent. For some parents the child represents an extension of self, and parental expectations are influenced by personal goals desired for themselves. Acknowledgment of such displaced emphasis can be stressful and painful to the parent, not easily recognized and accepted. In such cases the results of assessment may be denied or viewed as inaccurate, or in some cases questions may be raised regarding the assessor's competence.

On the other hand, a parent may be unable to hear what is said because of unrelenting hope, or guilt, or inability to cope. Reality appears too devastating. In these instances plans must be set down to help the parents, to give them concrete steps that they can take toward assisting the child and themselves toward a more satisfactory adjustment. A general review of the effect of the child's problem on the entire family constellation may need to be discussed—a delicate task rightfully falling to the social worker in charge of the case.

An assessor wisely maintains open channels to parental concerns, consistently questioning with them those self-care skills which require priority within the home setting. Such discussions with parents provide dialogue and, when necessary, allow the assessor to explain the sequence for developing skills, enumerating those subskills which need to be established before adequate independence in a task is attainable. Expectations can thus be kept more realistic.

An assessor progressively acquires skill and with experience internalizes a concept of his professional role. At such a point he is ready to serve as a model to parents, to demonstrate through his teaching, technical skill, and social interaction a number of specific ways for fostering independence in the child. The assessor's own anxiety is gradually absorbed through immersion in his helping role.

14 *Concluding remarks*

Independence is a lifelong process involving all developmental systems. The state of independence is not static, and each individual is both dependent and independent, wavering in degree according to internal and external forces at any one time.

Good assessment of functional abilities in self-care begins with a refined tool for eliciting specific data. Skillful technique is required for administering the assessment, and broad knowledge is needed in interpreting the results and compiling realistic, practical recommendations. The child must be viewed not only on the basis of his performance during the evaluation but also as an entity within his family constellation and as a member of his community and society at large.

Although "therapy" is not a subject of this handbook, certain treatment principles become evident, primarily ones relating to motor function, and these should be cited in the following concluding remarks:

- Therapy should be carried out in an orderly progression of steps, consistent with the sequences of development.
- Postural stability provides the foundation for voluntary movement, and cocontraction proceeds from the midline to the periphery.
- Therapy to establish motor control should progress from head to foot, proximally to distally.
- Gross motor tasks are accomplished before those requiring fine motor skills.
- Primitive reflexes are integrated before there is refined voluntary control.
- Equilibrium and other adaptive protective reactions are needed to adjust to the forces of gravity.
- The child learns by repetition, through redoing motor tasks again and again, while gradually modifying and perfecting his skill. When new motor patterns are introduced through therapy, the same process is required to achieve automatic control. At the same time repetition must be made interesting, and tasks should be introduced through various modalities, always shifting from one to the other before interest wanes.

The necessity of building substructures of function so that the child can master progressively complex tasks in self-care applies to the other developmental systems. This is borne out by Erikson's (1963) analysis of ego development in "eight stages of man," by Havighurst's (1952) organization of development tasks and education objectives, by Piaget and Inhelder's (1969) theories of human intellectual development, and by Ayres's (1964) hypothesized sequence of perceptual motor development.

Students and young therapists coming into the field have a part to play in testing theories that are in the process of validation and of substantiating the results of approaches now being carried out in clinical practice. There is exciting work ahead.

Taken in perspective, this handbook emerges as a clinician's attempt to help bridge the distance between didactic information and practical application of theory in working with children. Although it presents a framework for acquiring technical skill in assessing activities of daily living, more importantly, it points toward requisites for professional competence.

REFERENCES

Ayres, A. J. 1964. Perceptual-motor training for children. In Approaches to the treatment of patients with neuromuscular dysfunction. Dubuque, William C. Brown Co., Publishers.

Erikson, E. H. 1963. Childhood and society, ed. 2. New York, W. W. Norton & Co., Inc., Publishers.

Havighurst, R. 1952. Developmental tasks and education. New York, David McKay Co., Inc.

Piaget, J. and Inhelder, B. 1969. The psychology of the child. New York, Basic Books, Inc., Publishers.

Reflexes and reactions found in the handbook

Present at	B	1	2	3	4	5	6	7	8	9	10	11	12	2	3	4	5	6	Life
				MONTHS											YEARS				
Palmar grasp	■	■	■	■															
Moro	■	■	■	■															
Asymmetrical tonic neck		■	■	■															
Symmetrical tonic neck		■	■			■	■	■											
Labyrinthine righting																			
Prone			■	■	■	■	■	■	■	■	■	■	■	■	■	■	■	■	■
Supine					■	■	■	■	■	■	■	■	■	■	■	■	■	■	■
Optical righting																			
Prone			■	■	■	■	■	■	■	■	■	■	■	■	■	■	■	■	■
Supine						■	■	■	■	■	■	■	■	■	■	■	■	■	■
Tilting						■	■	■	■	■	■	■	■	■	■	■	■	■	■
Neck righting	■	■	■	■	■	■													
Body righting						■	■	■	■	■	■	■	■	■	■				
Landau					■	■	■	■	■	■	■	■	■	■					
Parachute and propping reactions																			
Forward							■	■	■	■	■	■	■	■	■	■	■	■	■
Sideward								■	■	■	■	■	■	■	■	■	■	■	■
Backward										■	■	■	■	■	■	■	■	■	■
Equilibrium reactions																			
Prone						■	■	■	■	■	■	■	■	■	■	■	■	■	■
Supine							■	■	■	■	■	■	■	■	■	■	■	■	■
Sitting								■	■	■	■	■	■	■	■	■	■	■	■
Standing													■	■	■	■	■	■	■
Oral reflexes																			
Rooting	■	■	■	■															
Sucking-swallowing	■	■	■	■	■														
Bite	■	■	■	■	■	■													
Gag—anterior two thirds	■	■	■	■	■	■	■												
—posterior one third	■	■	■	■	■	■	■	■	■	■	■	■	■	■	■	■	■	■	■
Present at	B	1	2	3	4	5	6	7	8	9	10	11	12	2	3	4	5	6	Life
				MONTHS											YEARS				

Definitions of activities

Activity of daily living	Developmental sequence Yr. Mo.	Definition of task
BED		
1. Supine position	Birth	Ability to lie on back
2. Prone position	Birth	Ability to lie on stomach
3. Roll to side	1-4 wk.	Ability to roll from back to side lying, reflexive
4. Roll prone to supine	0.6	Ability to roll from stomach to back; deliberate rolling
5. Roll supine to prone	0.7	Ability to roll from back to stomach; deliberate rolling
6. Sit up	0.10	Ability to attain sitting position
7. Propped sitting	0.6	Ability to sit with trunk erect, head and chin lifted, back supported
8. Sitting/hands props	0.7	Ability to sit alone passively without support, hands acting as accessory props
9. Sitting unsupported	0.10-0.12	Ability to sit unsupported indefinitely, hands and arms freed for manipulatory duty, eyes elevated
Reaching		
10. To midline	0.5	Ability to bring hands together at center of body and grasp object with two-handed approach from supine position
11. To mouth and face	0.6	Ability to grasp and bring object to mouth or face in sitting position
12. Above head	—	Ability to reach above head with both arms alternately, maintaining trunk stability in sitting position
13. Behind head	—	Ability to reach behind head with both arms alternately, maintaining trunk stability, hands together for manipulatory duty in sitting position
14. Behind back	—	Ability to reach behind back with both arms alternately, maintaining trunk stability, hands brought together for manipulatory duty

☐Inquiries on the Activities of Daily Living Assessment forms should be directed to the Occupational Therapy Department, Children's Hospital at Stanford, Palo Alto, Calif. 94304.

Activity of daily living	Developmental sequence Yr. Mo.	Definition of task
15. To toes	—	Ability to reach forward with both hands alternately when sitting to touch toes, hands free for manipulatory duty; may lean forward on elbows
FEEDING		
16. Swallow (liquids)	Birth	Ability to gather up food, squeeze it to back wall of throat, thereby stimulating swallowing reflex
17. Drooling under control	1.0	
18. Suck and use straw	2.0	
19. Chew (semi-solids, solids)	1.6	Ability to masticate solids by well-defined chewing
20. Finger foods	0.10	Ability to reach, grasp, and bring finger food to mouth
Utensils		Ability to grasp utensil, fill with food, and raise it to mouth without spilling
21. Bottle	0.10	
22. Spoon	3.0	
23. Cup	1.6	
24. Glass	2.0	
25. Fork	3.0	
26. Knife	6.0-7.0	
TOILETING		
27. Bowel control	1.6	Ability to regulate bowels so elimination occurs when seated on toilet
28. Bladder control	2.0	Ability to maintain sphincter control, remaining dry day and night
29. Sit on toilet	2.9	Ability to climb on lavatory seat unaided
30. Arrange clothing	4.0	Ability to manage fastenings, get pants up and down, hold dress away from buttocks
31. Cleanse self	5.0	
32. Flush toilet	3.3-5.0	
HYGIENE		
33. Turn faucets on/off	3.0	
34. Wash/dry hands/face	4.9	Ability to wash and dry hands and face efficiently without reminder of technique

Activity of daily living	Developmental sequence Yr. Mo.	Definition of task
HYGIENE—cont'd		
35. Wash ears	8.0	
36. Bathing	8.0	Ability to care for all needs when bathing
37. Deodorant	12.0-	
38. Care for teeth	4.9	Ability to combine all operations—prepare, brush, rinse
39. Care for nose	6.0	Ability to blow nose without assistance
40. Care for hair	7.6	Ability to comb and brush, check style with mirror
41. Care for nails	8.0	Ability to scrub and file nails
42. Feminine hygiene	Puberty	
UNDRESSING **Lower body**		
43. Untie shoe bow	2.0-3.0	
44. Remove shoes	2.0-3.0	Ability to untie shoe bow and remove shoes
45. Remove socks	1.6	
46. Remove pull-down garment	2.6	
Upper body		
47. Remove pullover garment	4.0	
DRESSING **Lower body**		
48. Put on socks	4.0	
49. Put on pull-down garment	4.0	Ability to put on garment, right side out, front and back correctly placed
50. Put on shoe	4.0	Ability to put shoe on correct foot
51. Lace shoe	5.0	
52. Tie bow	6.0	
Upper body		
53. Put on pullover garment	5.0	
FASTENERS **Unfastening** *Button*		
54. Front	3.0	
55. Side	3.0	
56. Back	5.6	

Activity of daily living	Developmental sequence Yr. Mo.	Definition of task
Zipper		
57. Front	3.3	
58. Separating front	3.6	
59. Back	4.9	
Buckle		
60. Belt	3.9	
61. Shoe	3.9	
Tie		
62. Back sash	5.0	
Fastening		
Button		
63. Large front	2.6	
64. Series of three	3.6	
65. Back	6.3	
Zipper		
66. Front, lock tab	4.0	
67. Separating	4.6	
68. Back	5.6	
Buckle		
69. Belt	4.0	
70. Shoe	4.0	
71. Insert belt in loops	4.6	
Tie		
72. Front	6.0	
73. Back	8.0	
74. Necktie	10.0	
Snaps		
75. Front	3.0	
76. Back	6.0	

References for activities

References for the developmental sequences have been selected on the basis of this handbook's description of the task and whether the description assists in setting down a definition of the task.

Developmental sequences have been compiled from both standardized and nonstandardized material. The purpose of listing the sequences in chronological, as well as descriptive form, is to aid the assessor in maintaining the order of the data.

Activity of daily living	Developmental sequence Yr. Mo.	Reference
BED		
1. Supine position	Birth	Bobath
2. Prone position	Birth	Bobath
3. Roll to side	1-4 wk.	Fiorentino
4. Roll prone to supine	0.6	Gesell
5. Roll supine to prone	0.7	Gesell
6. Sit up	0.10	Fiorentino and Illingworth
7. Propped sitting	0.6	Illingworth
8. Sitting/hands props	0.7	Gesell and Illingworth
9. Sitting unsupported	0.10-0.12	Gesell
Reaching		
10. To midline	0.5	Illingworth (includes two-handed approach and grasp)
11. To mouth and face	0.6	Gesell (in sitting position)
12. Above head	—	
13. Behind head	—	
14. Behind back	—	
15. To toes	1.3	Gesell
FEEDING		
16. Swallow (liquids)	Birth	Blockley, Miller
17. Drooling under control	1.0	Gesell
18. Suck and use straw	2.0	Miscellaneous forms
19. Chew (semisolids, solids)	1.6	Gesell
20. Finger foods	0.10	Gesell

Activity of daily living	Developmental sequence	Reference
	Yr. Mo.	

Utensils

21. Bottle	0.10	Gesell
22. Spoon	3.0	Gesell
23. Cup	1.6	Gesell
24. Glass	2.0	Gesell
25. Fork	3.0	Miscellaneous forms
26. Knife	6.0-7.0	Monterey Pupil Developmental Progress Scale*

TOILETING

27. Bowel control	1.6	Gesell
28. Bladder control	2.0	Gesell
29. Sit on toilet	2.9	Monterey Pupil Developmental Progress Scale
30. Arrange clothing	4.0	Gesell
31. Cleanse self	5.0	Gesell
32. Flush toilet	3.3-5.0	Monterey Pupil Developmental Progress Scale

HYGIENE

33. Turn faucets on/off	3.0	Miscellaneous forms
34. Wash/dry hands/face	4.9	Monterey Pupil Developmental Progress Scale
35. Wash ears	8.0	Miscellaneous forms
36. Bathing	8.0	Monterey Pupil Developmental Progress Scale
37. Deodorant	12.0-	
38. Care for teeth	4.9	Monterey Pupil Developmental Progress Scale
39. Care for nose	6.0	Monterey Pupil Developmental Progress Scale
40. Care for hair	7.6	Monterey Pupil Developmental Progress Scale
41. Care for nails	8.0	Monterey Pupil Developmental Progress Scale
42. Feminine hygiene	Puberty	

*The Monterey Pupil Developmental Progress Scale is a comprehensive list of 663 items covering performance in motor development, social/emotional development, cognitive skills, communication, self-help skills, practical skills, and individual expression. Permission to use excerpts is granted by the Comprehensive Coordinated Curriculum, Special Education Department, Monterey County Office of Education, Salinas, Calif.

Continued.

Activity of daily living	Developmental sequence Yr. Mo.	Reference
UNDRESSING		
Lower body		
43. Untie shoe bow	2.0-3.0	Miscellaneous forms
44. Remove shoes	2.0-3.0	Gesell
45. Remove socks	1.6	Gesell, Illingworth
46. Remove pull-down garment	2.6	Monterey Pupil Developmental Progress Scale
Upper body		
47. Remove pullover garment	4.0	Monterey Pupil Developmental Progress Scale
DRESSING		
Lower body		
48. Put on socks	4.0	Gesell
49. Put on pull-down garment	4.0	Monterey Pupil Developmental Progress Scale
50. Put on shoe	4.0	Gesell
51. Lace shoe	4.0-5.0	Gesell
52. Tie bow	6.0	Monterey Pupil Developmental Progress Scale
Upper body		
53. Put on pullover garment	5.0	Monterey Pupil Developmental Progress Scale
FASTENERS		
Unfastening		
Button		
54. Front	3.0	Monterey Pupil Developmental Progress Scale
55. Side	3.0	Monterey Pupil Developmental Progress Scale
56. Back	5.6	Monterey Pupil Developmental Progress Scale
Zipper		
57. Front	3.3	Monterey Pupil Developmental Progress Scale
58. Separating front	3.6	Monterey Pupil Developmental Progress Scale
59. Back	4.9	Monterey Pupil Developmental Progress Scale

Activity of daily living	Developmental sequence	Reference
	Yr. Mo.	
Buckle		
60. Belt	3.9	Monterey Pupil Developmental Progress Scale
61. Shoe	3.9	Monterey Pupil Developmental Progress Scale
Tie		
62. Back sash	5.0	Monterey Pupil Developmental Progress Scale
Fastening		
Button		
63. Large front	2.6	Monterey Pupil Developmental Progress Scale
64. Series	3.6	Monterey Pupil Developmental Progress Scale
65. Back	6.3	Monterey Pupil Developmental Progress Scale
Zipper		
66. Front, lock tab	4.0	Monterey Pupil Developmental Progress Scale
67. Separating	4.6	Monterey Pupil Developmental Progress Scale
Zipper		
68. Back	5.6	Monterey Pupil Developmental Progress Scale
Buckle		
69. Belt	4.0	Monterey Pupil Developmental Progress Scale
70. Shoe	4.0	Monterey Pupil Developmental Progress Scale
71. Insert belt in loops	4.6	Monterey Pupil Developmental Progress Scale
Tie		
72. Front	6.0	Monterey Pupil Developmental Progress Scale
73. Back	8.0	Monterey Pupil Developmental Progress Scale
74. Necktie	10.0	Monterey Pupil Developmental Progress Scale

Continued.

Activity of daily living	Developmental sequence Yr. Mo.	Reference
FASTENERS—cont'd		
Snaps		
75. Front	3.0	Monterey Pupil Developmental Progress Scale
76. Back	6.0	Monterey Pupil Developmental Progress Scale

Index